SECOND EDITION

Well Said

Pronunciation for Clear Communication

LINDA GRANT

HEINLE & HEINLE

THOMSON LEARNING

United States   Australia   Canada   Mexico   Singapore   Spain   United Kingdom

HEINLE & HEINLE

THOMSON LEARNING

Vice President,
Editorial Director ESL/EFL:
Nancy Leonhardt

Acquisitions Editor:
Eric Bredenberg

Developmental Editor:
Thomas Healy

Sr. Production Editor:
Maryellen E. Killeen

Marketing Manager:
Charlotte Sturdy

Sr. Manufacturing Coordinator:
Mary Beth Hennebury

Production/Composition:
Laurel Technical Services

Cover Design:
Carole Rollins

Cover Image:
© 2000 Estate of Alexander
Calder/Artists Rights Society
(ARS), New York

Printer/Binder:
Phoenix Book

Library of Congress
Cataloging-in-Publication
Data
Grant, Linda.
Well said : pronunciation for clear
communication/Linda Grant.-2nd ed.
p. cm.
ISBN 0-8384-0208-9
1. English language—Pronunciation.
1. Title.
PE1137.W63   2000
428.3'4—dc21   00-039725

For more information, contact Heinle
& Heinle Publishers, 20 Park Plaza,
Boston, MA 02116.

For permission to use material from
this text or product, contact us by
Tel   (800) 730-2214
Fax   (800) 730-2215
www.thomsonrights.com

This book is printed on
acid-free paper.

ASIA (including India):
Thomson Learning
60 Albert Street, #15-01
Albert Complex
Singapore 189969
Tel   65 336-6411
Fax   65 336-7411

AUSTRALIA/NEW ZEALAND:
Nelson
102 Dodds Street
South Melbourne
Victoria 3205
Australia
Tel   61 (0)3 9685-4111
Fax   61 (0)3 9685-4199

LATIN AMERICA:
Thomson Learning
Seneca 53
Colonia Polanco
11560 Mexico, D.F. Mexico
Tel   (525) 281-2906
Fax   (525) 281-2656

CANADA:
Nelson
1120 Birchmount Road
Toronto, Ontario
Canada M1K 5G4
Tel   (416) 752-9100
Fax   (416) 752-8102

UK/EUROPE/MIDDLE EAST/AFRICA:
Thomson Learning
Birkshire House
168-173 High Holborn
London WC1V 7AA
United Kingdom
Tel   44 (0)171 497-1422
Fax   44 (0)171 497-1426

SPAIN (includes Portugal):
Paraninfo
Calle Magallanes 25
28015 Madrid
España
Tel   34 (0)91 446-3350
Fax   34 (0)91 445-6218

Contents

Appendixes   Page

To the Instructor

Welcome to the second edition of *Well Said*, a text designed to improve the speech intelligibility of high intermediate to advanced learners of American English. The text was written for the general ESL/EFL population but should be especially useful to those who wish to communicate more clearly in academic, business, scientific, and professional settings.

Well Said, Second Edition, addresses the pronunciation needs of students from a variety of language backgrounds. The body of the text focuses on sound/spelling patterns, syllables, word endings, linking, stress, rhythm, and intonation problems common to students of most language backgrounds. The appendixes provide individualized practice for consonant and vowel problems, which vary widely in most groups of students.

The text adapts to a variety of learning formats—large class, small group, independent learning, and tutorials. The interactive nature of many practices in Chapters 1 through 10, however, makes the text especially well suited for classroom use. The accompanying audio program encourages independent practice and self-study as well. The consonant and vowel practices in the appendixes are designed for independent laboratory use but are also effective with groups of students in the classroom.

The first edition of *Well Said* was written in response to problems the pronunciation instructor in today's classroom faces:

- Individualizing the pronunciation curriculum to meet the diverse needs of a group of learners

- Guiding learners into natural, relevant communicative contexts so that carryover of pronunciation into speaking is not left entirely to chance

- Establishing realistic goals and reasonable measures of progress that account for destabilization during learning, different rates of acquisition, and the role of the learner in evaluation and monitoring

- Identifying an integrated pronunciation curriculum that precludes the need for heavy supplements of teacher-made materials or texts from other skill areas

In response to these problems, *Well Said, Second Edition,* continues to offer the following distinctive features:

- Introductory chapter for assessing individual needs and priorities

- Progression from controlled practice into relevant, naturalistic communicative contexts

- Peer monitoring, independent practice, and self-evaluation

- Integration of pronunciation with listening and discourse-level speaking formats

- Emphasis on stress, rhythm, and intonation, as well as on individual speech sounds

- Appendixes with an overview of consonants and vowels and intensive practice with the more troublesome sounds

- Activities that maximize student talking time and provide sufficient practice to enable students to assimilate elements of clear speech into oral communication

Special Features of the Second Edition

You will find these changes in this second edition of *Well Said*:

- Additional strategies (A Helpful Hint) for long-term pronunciation improvement
- Homework (Prime-Time Practice) and real-world practice (Beyond the Pronunciation Classroom)
- Updated vocabulary and communicative activities
- Increased emphasis on a multisensory (visual, auditory, physical, and kinesthetic) approach to pronunciation learning
- Index to the text
- Audio program indexed to the chapters

Organization of the Text

The text is organized around features of pronunciation. Each pronunciation point is integrated with listening activities and speaking formats that move from structured to more spontaneous tasks.

The text has 10 chapters and three appendixes. Chapter 1 contains a diagnostic instrument and tools for learner self-evaluation and goal setting. These instruments motivate students, yield valuable individual and class profiles, and alert the instructor to the parts of the book that need emphasis. Chapter 2 explores the dictionary for pronunciation purposes and introduces pronunciation points covered in detail in later chapters. Chapter 3 clarifies key sound/spelling patterns in English and provides concentrated practice with final consonant sounds. Chapter 4 covers syllables and grammatical endings. Chapters 5 through 10 address stress, rhythm, and intonation. While working through the chapters, instructors can refer to the consonant and vowel overviews in the Appendixes as needed.

Sequential movement through the chapters will result in a coherent presentation of the features of clear speaking. Instructors can, however, establish their own priorities and set alternative paths through the material. For example, consonants and vowels can be presented before or after the core chapters on stress, rhythm, and intonation. Instructors can delete or extend speaking activities, depending on the needs and interests of the class, whether it be quarter-, semester-, or workshop-length. Considerations in reordering chapters are in the *Instructor's Manual*.

Organization Within Chapters

Except for the first two introductory chapters, all chapters follow a similar progression.

Each chapter begins with a section called "Listen!" designed to enhance aural awareness of the target feature in each chapter and to build skills for peer and self-monitoring.

In the next section, "Rules and Practices," students discover pronunciation *rules* and regularities. Structured and semistructured *practices* help students gain control of pronunciation features before applying them in more challenging communicative contexts.

In "Communicative Practice," learners incorporate pronunciation concepts into contextualized speaking activities that elicit, as naturally as possible, numerous instances of the teaching point. These activities guide learners as they bridge the gap between a focus on accuracy and a focus on meaning.

"Extend Your Skills . . ." recycles target pronunciation features into discourse-level speaking formats (graph explanation, problem solving, discussion, contrastive analysis, and process presentation). This section includes suggestions for audiotaping, videotaping, and self-evaluation.

"Prime-Time Practice" assigns taped homework for valuable out-of-class practice. These assignments incorporate self-monitoring and, in some cases, teacher feedback. Most chapters wind down with "Oral Review," which students can complete as either a final review or an end-of-chapter quiz.

As students become more comfortable with new pronunciation patterns, Chapters 6 through 10 conclude with "Beyond the Pronunciation Classroom." This segment helps students rehearse and transfer pronunciation accuracy into everyday communication with native speakers.

The chapters contain brief features called *Something to Think About* and *A Helpful Hint*. Under these headings are incentives and strategies for pronunciation practice.

Appendixes B and C contain an overview of all consonants and vowels, as well as intensive practice with the most troublesome sounds. The consonant and vowel sections contain listening and practice exercises for individual and small-group use and "Communicative Practice" for in-class reviews or out-of-class small-group work. The answer keys for Appendixes B and C are at the end of the text.

The vocabulary in the lessons is challenging and pertinent to various academic and work settings. Discussion of vocabulary can be a valuable part of each lesson. Students have opportunities throughout the text to personalize vocabulary and to practice terms from their fields of work or study.

Finally, the text encourages the learner to be actively involved in the process of becoming a clear speaker of English and the instructor to guide this process.

Instructor's Manual

The *Instructor's Manual* supports novice and experienced pronunciation instructors with teaching suggestions, theoretical underpinnings, rationale for activities, and additional exercises. It also includes answer keys, audio tapescripts for Chapters 1 through 10, and a list of references.

Audio Program

The audio program enables students to work through the text independently and to obtain additional out-of-class practice. Instructors can use the recorded material in the classroom at their discretion.

Progress in Pronunciation Improvement

Although more research is needed in pronunciation learning in a second or foreign language, here are characteristics of pronunciation development you may notice:

- Individual variation will occur in the rate and extent of pronunciation improvement. Progress may be influenced by such factors as motivation, aptitude, personality, nature of the first language, language learning strategies, and amount of English spoken outside class.

- New pronunciation skills are acquired over time. In the beginning stages, use of a new skill will require conscious attention. Over time and with practice, skills may become more automatic. New skills often manifest themselves in controlled speaking or reading activities before they are apparent in spontaneous speech. New skills may be most difficult to incorporate when the communicative/cognitive demands on the learner are heavy.

- Errors are an expected and natural part of the learning process. Learners might approximate features before they can produce them clearly. They may overgeneralize patterns before refining them. They may lose former skills while acquiring new ones. In short, incorrect productions sometimes indicate that learning is occurring.

- Learners might only partially integrate new pronunciation features into spontaneous speech. However, even partial integration of a new pronunciation skill has a positive overall effect on intelligibility.

As our knowledge of pronunciation development in a second language grows in the years ahead, I hope this text serves as an effective guide for enhancing pronunciation skills in authentic communication. I appreciate hearing from users of *Well Said, Second Edition.* If you have comments about this edition, please forward them to me through the publisher.

Linda Grant

To the Student

One of the most difficult aspects of learning another language is mastering the pronunciation. Many of you can read, write, and understand American English well, but you may face situations in which your pronunciation interferes with clear and effective communication. This textbook/audio program is designed to help you improve your pronunciation so that you can communicate confidently and be understood with relative ease.

In this course, you will focus on those pronunciation issues that are common problems for high intermediate to advanced learners of American English. Practices include both structured exercises and real-life communication activities. The arrangement of activities gives you an opportunity to gain control of new pronunciation skills before practicing them in the types of situations you might encounter every day at work or school. As you progress through the activities in each chapter, your pronunciation of new patterns will gradually require less conscious attention and become more automatic.

Throughout the course, you will work individually and with partners, small groups, and the whole class. You will have many chances to engage in the roles of both speaker and listener/monitor. As a listener, you will develop the ability to hear the differences between clear and unclear pronunciation forms in the speech of your classmates. You will also strengthen the all-important ability to monitor and correct your own pronunciation.

Here are a few more points to consider as you begin this course in pronunciation improvement:

- Mistakes are a natural, necessary part of the process of improving pronunciation skills, so don't be afraid of them.

- You probably won't eliminate your accent or speak with 100 percent accuracy. A more realistic goal is to change those aspects of your pronunciation that interfere with your ability to be understood clearly. You do not need to sound like a native speaker of American English to be fully and easily understood.

- Your attitude is an important element in pronunciation improvement. You will make more progress if you are strongly motivated to improve.

- You will make more progress in pronunciation improvement if you practice your English outside the classroom and in real speaking situations.

I hope *Well Said, Second Edition* helps you in your efforts to become a clear speaker of American English.

ACKNOWLEDGMENTS

Of the many people who have contributed to this book, I am most grateful to Laura and Richard Kretschmer, Judy Gilbert, Joan Morley, Rita Wong, David Mendelsohn, and Bill Acton—teachers and colleagues who have prodded my thinking about speech/pronunciation teaching and learning.

These readers and reviewers deserve special thanks: Karen Tucker and C. A. Johnston (Georgia Institute of Technology), Beverly Beisbier (University of Southern California), Kathleen Flynn (Glendale College), Melinda Kodimer (UCLA), Lois Lanier (University of Maryland), Scott Stevens (University of Delaware), and Ramon Valenzuela (Harvard University). For helping me see the strengths and weaknesses of the first edition, I thank the many unnamed reviewers and owe a special debt to Cathleen Jacobson (Georgia Institute of Technology) for her extensive comments.

I am also grateful to my editors at Heinle & Heinle and especially to the senior production editor, Maryellen Eschmann-Killeen; to my students for demonstrating over the years that the combination of motivated learners and effective teaching and learning strategies can make a difference; and, last but not least, to my husband and daughters for understanding and support.

Your Pronunciation Profile

A *pronunciation profile* is a general description of your pronunciation abilities and needs. It is *not* a test. The purpose of a profile is to alert you and your teacher to the parts of this book that will be of most help to you and to the class.

The speaking activities in the first part of this chapter form the basis of your profile. The activities are ordered from easy to more difficult and from structured to more spontaneous.

The pronunciation profile has three parts:

Part A: Paragraph Reading

Part B: Short Responses to Interview Questions

Part C: Peer Introductions

Do as many of the activities as you have time for. The more speaking you do, the more accurately your teacher will be able to evaluate your pronunciation strengths and weaknesses.

During all the speaking activities in this chapter, your teacher can use the "Speech Profile Summary Form" on page 4 to record observations. At the end of the course, you can repeat "Part A: Paragraph Reading" to measure improvement.

The Speech Profile

Part A: Paragraph Reading

Choose one of the three following paragraphs. Read it silently for meaning. Then read it out loud as naturally as possible. You can (1) record the paragraph and submit the cassette to your teacher or (2) read the paragraph in an individual consultation with your teacher.

Reading 1

Have you ever watched young children practice the sounds of the language they are learning? They imitate, repeat, and sing consonant and vowel combinations without effort. For young children, learning to speak a language is natural and automatic. No one would suspect that complex learning is occurring. For adult learners, however, pronunciation of a new language is not automatic. It presents an unusual challenge. Why is pronunciation progress in adults more limited? Some researchers say the reasons are biological or physical. Others say they are social or cultural. Although many questions are still unanswered, it is important to realize two things about clear speaking. First, pronunciation improvement might be difficult, but it *is* possible. Second, adults can learn to communicate clearly in English without losing their accents or their identification with their native cultures.

Reading 2*

Have you observed the ways people from different cultures use silence? Have you noticed that some people interrupt conversations more than other people? All cultures do not have the same rules governing these areas of communication. Many Americans interpret silence in conversations to mean disapproval, disagreement, or unsuccessful communication. They often try to fill silence by saying something even if they have nothing to say! On the other hand, Americans don't appreciate a person who dominates a conversation. Knowing when to take turns in a conversation in another language can sometimes cause difficulty. Should you wait until someone has finished a sentence before contributing to a discussion, or can you break into the middle of someone's sentence? Interrupting someone who is speaking is considered rude in the United States. Even children are taught explicitly not to interrupt.

*From Deena R. Levine and Mara B. Adelman, *Beyond Language: Intercultural Communication for English as a Second Language* (Englewood Cliffs, N.J.: Prentice Hall, 1982), p. 23. Reprinted with permission.

Reading 3*

Edward T. Hall is a famous anthropologist who thinks that different cultures have different outlooks on time, space, and personal relationships. He classifies cultures along a continuum ranging from high context to low context. In high-context cultures, the circumstances surrounding a message carry more meaning than the message itself. For example, if an individual negotiates a business agreement, the reputation of the family is considered. Verbal promises are trusted, so there is little paperwork. What about low-context cultures? In low-context cultures, the words themselves are more important than the context. Social and family connections are not always regarded. Because the contract itself is the most important part of an agreement, the agreement might generate a lot of legal paperwork. Can you think of other examples of how cultural differences might lead to miscommunication?

*Information adapted from Edward T. Hall, *The Hidden Dimension* (Anchor Books, 1990).

Part B: Short Responses to Interview Questions

Record brief responses to these questions or schedule an individual meeting with your teacher. Do not write or rehearse your answers. Speak as naturally as possible for about two minutes.

1. What is your educational background and/or your work history?
2. What is your purpose for studying English?
3. How much English do you speak each day? In what situations do you speak it?
4. What do you hope to achieve in this class?
5. What do you hope to be doing in five years?

Part C: Peer Introductions

In class, work in pairs with a person whom you do not know well. Spend a few minutes interviewing and getting to know your partner. Take brief notes. Use your notes to introduce your partner to the class.

Speech Profile Summary Form

Name: _____ Date: _____

The speaking activities in this chapter indicate that you need to concentrate on the following pronunciation points.

Elements of Speech	Difficulties	Examples
Consonants (Chapter 3; Appendix B)		
Vowels (Appendix C)		
Syllables and Grammatical Endings (Chapter 4)		
Stress in Words (Chapters 5 and 6)		
Rhythm in Sentences (Chapter 7)		
Focus and Special Emphasis (Chapter 8)		
Intonation/Pitch Patterns (Chapters 8 and 9)		
Thought Groups and Linking (Chapter 10)		
Delivery (rate of speech, loudness, eye contact, posture, movement, and gestures):		

THREE PRONUNCIATION STRENGTHS:

1. _____

2. _____

3. _____

THREE PRONUNCIATION PRIORITIES (elements most in need of practice):

1. _____

2. _____

3. _____

SOMETHING TO THINK ABOUT

You might be having trouble with **consonants and vowels.** Or you might be struggling with **stress, rhythm, and intonation.** Both areas can affect how well you are understood. If you have limited time to work on pronunciation, however, focus on your priorities—pronunciation features that will improve your speech the most.

A priority might be an error that is especially frequent. Or it might be a feature that has a greater impact on overall intelligibility. For most students, problems with consonants and vowels affect how well the listener understands words. Problems with stress, rhythm, and intonation, however, can affect the understanding of phrases, sentences, and even whole conversations!

Needs and Attitudes Assessment

This self-assessment is a tool to encourage you to think about your speaking needs and to help your teacher design a course to meet those needs. Read each item and answer both A and B. After you complete the items, discuss the results in small groups of four or five students and report the results to the class.

Tasks	A. How important is this in your work/studies? (1 = not at all . . . 4 = very)	B. What is your ability in this area? (1 = poor . . . 4 = good)
1. Participating in informal conversations		
2. Participating in discussions		
3. Managing group discussions		
4. Giving short presentations		
5. Giving long presentations		
6. Giving information or instructions		
What is your easiest speaking situation?		
What is your most difficult speaking situation?		

Skills	A. How important is this in your work/studies? (1 = not at all . . . 4 = very)	B. What is your ability in this area? (1 = poor . . . 4 = good)
1. Speaking clearly and confidently		
2. Speaking at a good speed		
3. Understanding rapid speech easily		
4. Using appropriate stress patterns in words		
5. Using appropriate rhythm patterns in sentences		
6. Using appropriate intonation or pitch patterns		
7. Using clear consonants		
8. Using clear vowels		
9. Using appropriate nonverbal communication (e.g., eye contact, gestures)		

In what areas above would you most like to improve?

Attitudes

1. Which features of English pronunciation appeal to you?

2. Which aspects do you not like? Why?

3. Look at the cartoon below. What does it depict? What are your preconceptions about pronunciation learning?

Drawing by
Linda Williams Dorage.
Reprinted by permission
of the artist.

Setting Personal Goals

How intelligible or capable of being understood are you? How intelligible do you need or want to be? Use the following *pronunciation proficiency continuum* to judge your own intelligibility. First, put a check (✓) at a point along the continuum to indicate your intelligibility or pronunciation proficiency *now*. Then put an asterisk (*) at a point along the continuum to indicate your pronunciation proficiency goal.

SOMETHING TO THINK ABOUT

When setting goals, be realistic. For most adult students of American English, achieving near-native pronunciation (position 6+ on the continuum) may not be realistic for the following reasons:

- **It may not be desirable.** Your accent is important because it identifies you with your native language and culture.

- **It may not be necessary.** You can speak American English clearly and be fully understood, yet still retain aspects of your accent.

- **It may not be possible.** Most adult learners have great difficulty eliminating all traces of accent.

Pronunciation Proficiency Continuum

```
1           2           3           4           5           6
|-----------|-----------|-----------|-----------|-----------|
```

1 Minimal pronunciation proficiency; listener understands only occasional words

2 Very difficult for listener to understand, even one accustomed to speaking with nonnative speakers; constant repetition needed

3 Somewhat intelligible to native speakers who are accustomed to speaking with nonnative speakers; frequent pronunciation variations distract the listener and prevent understanding

4 Intelligible to most native speakers; accent and pronunciation variations are somewhat distracting to the listener but rarely interfere with understanding

5 Obvious accent and pronunciation variations, but these do not interfere with understanding and rarely distract the listener

6 Barely detectable accent; pronunciation is almost like that of native speakers; rare, isolated mispronunciations, but no patterns of error

Keep the results of this proficiency continuum. Refer back to the scale midway through the course to reassess your goals.

The scale was adapted from (1) American Council on the Teaching of Foreign Languages (ACTFL), *Proficiency Guidelines* (Hastings-on-Hudson, N.Y.: ACTFL, 1986), by permission of ACTFL. See page 8 for a complete list of references; and from (2) Joan Morley, "EFL/ESL Intelligibility Index," *How Many Languages Do You Speak?* Nagoya Gakuin Daigaku: Gaikokugo Kyoiku Kiyo No. 19, Jan./Feb. 1988.

ACTFL REFERENCES

American Council on the Teaching of Foreign Languages. *Proficiency Guidelines.* Hastings-on-Hudson, N.Y.: ACTFL, 1986.

Draper, Jamie B. *State Initiatives and Activities in Foreign Languages and International Studies.* Monograph. Washington, D.C.: Joint National Committee for Languages, 1986.

_____. *The State of the States: State Initiatives in Foreign Languages and International Studies.* Monograph. Washington, D.C.: Joint National Committee for Languages, 1989.

Eddy, Peter A. "The Effect of Foreign Language Study in High School on Verbal Ability as Measured by the Scholastic Aptitude Test—Verbal." Washington, D.C.: Center for Applied Linguistics, 1981.

Masciantonio, Rudolph. "Tangible Benefits of the Study of Latin: A Review of Research." *Foreign Language Annals* 10 (1977): 376–377.

National Council of State Supervisors of Foreign Languages. *Distance Learning in Foreign Languages: A Position Paper with Guidelines.* Monograph. Washington, D.C.: National Council of State Supervisors of Foreign Languages, 1990.

New York State Board of Regents. *New York State Board of Regents Action Plan to Improve Elementary and Secondary Education Results.* Albany, N.Y.: University of the State of New York, State Education Department, 1984.

Panetta, Leon. "The Quiet Crisis of Global Competence." Northeast Conference *Newsletter* 30 (Fall 1991): 14–17.

Using a Dictionary for Pronunciation

"Hello, I'm Clifton (klĭf'tun) Latimer (lat'ĭ•mẽr)."

Introduction to Dictionary Symbols

A dictionary is a useful pronunciation resource, especially when you can anticipate the vocabulary needed for a discussion, class, meeting, or presentation. Dictionaries use special symbols to show pronunciation, but these symbols may be confusing because they vary from dictionary to dictionary. Dictionaries for English learners, like *The Newbury House Dictionary of American English,* use a modified version of the International Phonetic Alphabet (IPA). Most standard American English dictionaries use a different symbol system explained in a pronunciation key in the introduction and printed at the bottom of each page. This chapter will help you learn about *your* dictionary and the pronunciation symbols it uses.

1 **Syllables:** Each vowel sound in a word creates a beat, or syllable. Dictionaries separate syllables with spaces, dots (•), or hyphens (-). Write the number of syllables or beats in these words, according to your dictionary.

Say the words with your teacher or the speaker on tape.

WORD	NUMBER OF SYLLABLES
business	2
specific	3
president	3
learned (verb)	1
learned (adjective)	2
fatigue	2
family	3
serious	3

2 **Stress in Words:** Dictionaries usually indicate *primary stress*, the strongest syllable in a word, with a boldface mark (') above, in front of, or behind the stressed syllable. Secondary stress is usually indicated with a lighter mark (') or a lower mark (,). For pronunciation purposes, pay attention to primary stresses. Mark the primary stress in each of these words, according to your dictionary.

Say the words with your teacher or the speaker on tape.

'dem on strate	hy poth' e sis ✓
tech'nol o gy	'con duct (noun)
tech no 'log i cal	'con 'duct (verb)
'teen ag er	hu 'mid i ty

Where does *your* dictionary place the mark for primary stress? _____

Note: Syllable breaks for writing are usually indicated in the first entry word. Syllable breaks for pronunciation are usually indicated in parentheses or between slant lines (/). When dictionaries show more than one pronunciation in parentheses, the first is the most common.

3 **Vowels with Name Sounds:** These vowels, sometimes called *long vowels*, are pronounced like their letter names. Dictionaries show these vowels with phonetic symbols or macrons (–) over the vowels. Say the letter name of each vowel.

ā   ē   ī   ō   ū*

*ū is sometimes designated (yoo) in pronunciation keys.

Write the vowel symbol your dictionary uses for the italicized vowels in these words. Then find the key word for each symbol in the pronunciation key.

Repeat the words after your teacher or the speaker on tape.

	SYMBOL	KEY WORD
f*a*ce and m*ai*l	_____	_____
s*ea*t and m*ee*t	_____	_____
*ai*sle and m*igh*t	_____	_____
r*o*le and g*oa*l	_____	_____
*u*se and f*ue*l	_____	_____

4 **Vowels with Base Sounds:** These vowels are often called *short vowels*. Dictionaries show these vowels with phonetic symbols, vowel letters with breves (˘), or vowel letters with no marks above them. Write the symbols your dictionary uses for the italicized vowels in these words. Then find the key word for each symbol in the pronunciation key.

Repeat the words after your teacher or the speaker on tape.

	SYMBOL	KEY WORD
*a*d and m*a*gazine	_____	_____
y*e*s and exp*e*nse	_____	_____
*i*t and b*ui*lding	_____	_____
h*o*t and c*o*py	_____	_____
l*u*ck and an*o*ther	_____	_____

5 **The Schwa Sound:** The most common vowel sound in American English is the schwa /ə/, as in *a*bout. The schwa is generally used for vowel sounds in unstressed syllables.

Example: available = /ə • 'veʸl • ə • bəl/

Look up these words in your dictionary and underline the schwa /ə/ sounds.

Repeat the words after your teacher or the speaker on tape.

meth od	com plain
me thod i cal	ac a dem ic
com mon	pro duc tion

6 **Consonant Sounds:** Write the symbol your dictionary uses for the italicized letters in each set of words. Then find the key word for each symbol in the pronunciation key.

 Repeat the words after your teacher or the speaker on tape.

	SYMBOL	KEY WORD
*z*ero		
ra*z*or		
lo*s*e		
clo*s*e (verb)	_____	_____
*sh*ow		
tis*s*ue		
ini*t*ial		
spe*c*ial	_____	_____
*ch*eck		
na*t*ural		
fu*t*ure		
si*t*uation	_____	_____
divi*s*ion		
A*s*ian		
u*s*ual		
bei*g*e	_____	_____
*j*oke		
a*g*ent		
gra*d*uate		
sche*d*ule	_____	_____
ma*x*imum		
e*x*plain		
e*x*treme		
a*cc*ept	_____	_____

A HELPFUL HINT

You can improve your overall intelligibility in a discussion or presentation if you correct the pronunciation of just one or two key terms, especially if the terms occur over and over. Develop the habit of anticipating key vocabulary you will need for meetings, presentations, and discussions. Look up the words in your dictionary or ask native speakers to pronounce the words for you. If you ask native speakers to use the key terms in sentences, you will hear more natural pronunciations. You might even ask native speakers to record the words and sentences so that you can practice on tape.

Exercises

Exercise 1

Part A: Think about an upcoming class, meeting, presentation, conversation, or discussion. In the spaces below, write five words you expect to use and want to pronounce clearly. Write the dictionary pronunciations.

Example 1: Liliana is a graduate student in civil engineering. She looked at her notes for an upcoming class discussion, and these are some of the words she wrote down: *matrix, reliability, prefabricate.*

Example 2: Yu Huang is a full-time English student. He could not think of an upcoming situation, so he wrote words he had trouble with during a recent visit to the health center: *cough, headache, contagious.*

YOUR WORDS	DICTIONARY PRONUNCIATION
1.	
2.	
3.	
4.	
5.	

Part B: Write a typical phrase or sentence you might use with each of the words above. Say each sentence three times as naturally as possible. As you say each sentence, look up from your book and imagine that you are actually speaking to someone. Dictate your sentences to your partner.

Example: (contagious) _Is the virus contagious?_

1. _____
2. _____
3. _____
4. _____
5. _____

Exercise 2

Think about key technical or professional terms you often use at school or at work. Write the words below. Circle the words with pronunciations you are unsure of. Look up the circled words in your dictionary and write the pronunciation symbols for each word. Speak in slow motion and say each word once, then twice in a row, and then three times in a row.

KEY WORD LIST

	Key Word	**Dictionary Pronunciation**
Example:	*receipt*	/rə · ˈsiʸt/

1. _____ _____
2. _____ _____
3. _____ _____
4. _____ _____
5. _____ _____
6. _____ _____
7. _____ _____
8. _____ _____
9. _____ _____
10. _____ _____

Create a class list of hard-to-pronounce words by contributing one or two of the most difficult words from each of your lists.

Pronunciation Key for *Well Said*

The pronunciation symbols in this text are similar to the IPA symbols used in *The Newbury House Dictionary of American English* except for a few vowel sounds. Some symbols look like letters of the English alphabet; others do not. Each symbol is printed between slant lines (/) next to a familiar key word to help you pronounce the sound. Complete the chart by writing the symbol *your* dictionary uses for each sound.

Learn the key words. Listen and repeat after your teacher or the speaker on tape.

Consonant Symbols			
Key Word	**Well Said**	**Newbury Dictionary**	**Your Dictionary**
1. *p*ie	/p/	/p/	
2. *b*oy	/b/	/b/	
3. *t*en	/t/	/t/	
4. *d*ay	/d/	/d/	
5. *k*ey	/k/	/k/	
6. *g*o	/g/	/g/	
7. *f*ine	/f/	/f/	
8. *v*an	/v/	/v/	
9. *th*ink	/θ/	/θ/	
10. *th*ey	/ð/	/ð/	
11. *s*ee	/s/	/s/	
12. *z*oo	/z/	/z/	
13. *sh*oe	/ʃ/	/ʃ/	
14. mea*s*ure	/ʒ/	/ʒ/	
15. *ch*oose	/tʃ/	/tʃ/	
16. *j*ob	/dʒ/	/dʒ/	
17. *m*y	/m/	/m/	
18. *n*o	/n/	/n/	
19. si*ng*	/ŋ/	/ŋ/	
20. *l*et	/l/	/l/	
21. *r*ed	/r/	/r/	
22. *w*e	/w/	/w/	
23. *y*es	/y/	/y/	
24. *h*ome	/h/	/h/	

Key Word	Vowel Symbols		
	Well Said	*Newbury Dictionary*	*Your Dictionary*
1. h*e*	/iʸ/	/i/	
2. h*i*t	/ɪ/	/ɪ/	
3. m*ay*	/eʸ/	/eɪ/	
4. g*e*t	/ɛ/	/ɛ/	
5. m*a*d	/æ/	/æ/	
6. b*ir*d	/ɜr/	/ɜr/	
7. c*u*p	/ʌ/	/ʌ/	
*a*bout	/ə/	/ə/	
8. h*o*t, f*a*ther	/ɑ/	/ɑ/	
9. t*oo*	/uʷ/	/u/	
10. g*oo*d	/ʊ/	/ʊ/	
11. kn*ow*	/oʷ/	/oʊ/	
12. l*aw*	/ɔ/	/ɔ/	
13. f*i*ne	/aɪ/	/aɪ/	
14. n*ow*	/aʊ/	/aʊ/	
15. b*oy*	/ɔɪ/	/ɔɪ/	

Exercise 3

Look at the cartoon at the beginning of this chapter. It shows dictionary pronunciation symbols for the name *Clifton Latimer*. Write your first and last names below. Using phonetic symbols from *Well Said*, write the pronunciation of your name between the slant lines. Ask your partner to pronounce your name, using the symbols you wrote.

First Name: _____   /   /

Last Name: _____   /   /

Do any sounds in your name not exist in American English?

Exercise 4 (Optional)

If you want additional practice with the phonetic alphabet, place the symbol from *Well Said* next to the underlined sound in each word. Compare your answers with your partner's answers.

1. <u>ch</u>ild   _____   **6.** <u>g</u>ot   _____

2. ano<u>th</u>er   _____   **7.** <u>ea</u>sy   _____

3. ri<u>ng</u>   _____   **8.** p<u>ai</u>n   _____

4. tou<u>gh</u>   _____   **9.** <u>r</u>ight   _____

5. <u>c</u>razy   _____   **10.** c<u>oo</u>k   _____

Sound/Spelling Patterns

"I believe you're right, Professor. It is 'cat' before 'fish,' except after 'bird.'"

Drawing by Ralph L. Zamorano. Reprinted by permission of the artist.

One of the most confusing aspects of English pronunciation is spelling. Because English has been influenced by so many other languages, sound/spelling relationships are irregular. Notice how many different ways the letter *g* is pronounced in these words:

get   = /g/ as in **g**o

a**g**ent = /dʒ/ as in **j**ob

bei**g**e = /ʒ/ as in mea**su**re

Notice how many different spellings produce the same /ʃ/ sound as in **sh**oe:

share = /ʃ/	ra**ti**o = /ʃ/
so**ci**al = /ʃ/	a**ss**ure = /ʃ/
sugar = /ʃ/	ma**ch**ine = /ʃ/

Some pronunciation problems are related to difficulties recognizing sound/spelling patterns. This chapter will clarify some consonant sounds and spellings that are especially troublesome. For an overview of all the consonants of American English and practice with specific sounds, see Appendix B ("Consonants").

Listen!

Listen to your teacher or the speaker on tape present a short passage about the government of the United States. The first time, close your book and listen for meaning. The second time, focus on the sounds of the italicized spellings below.

American Government

Many interna*ti*onal students are confused about the government of the United States. They wonder who holds the power and who makes the deci*si*ons. Is the power si*tu*ated in the presiden*ti*al office or in the congre*ssi*onal offices?

The answers go back over two cen*tu*ries. Ever since the days of the American Revolu*ti*on, Americans have been suspi*ci*ous of government power. The early Americans believed that England had abused its power and restricted indivi*du*al freedoms. They also believed that the primary role of a na*ti*onal government should be to protect indivi*du*al freedom and to promote self-suffi*ci*ency.

Because of this suspi*ci*on of strong central governments, the writers of the Constitu*ti*on divided power among three branches of the government: the e*x*ecutive (the president), the legislative (the Congress), and the judi*ci*al branches. Although this divi*si*on may not be the most effi*ci*ent way to run a government, it prevents any one branch from obtaining too much power.

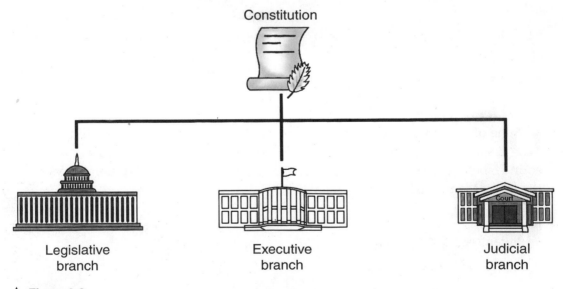

▲ Figure 3-2
Organization chart of the United States government.

This passage contained several unusual sound/spelling correspondences. Did you notice any patterns? In the next section, you will discover pronunciation rules for the italicized spellings.

Rules and Practices 1:
Unusual Consonant Spelling Patterns

The following spelling patterns are common in business, academic, medical, scientific, and technical terms. Like many rules of English, these patterns will be true *most* of the time, not *all* of the time.

Rule 3-1

The /ʃ/ sound is commonly spelled **sh** *as in* **sh**oe.

Listen to the italicized letters in the phrases below. Circle the sound you hear in each column. Do you hear . . .

/t/ or /ʃ/?	/s/ or /ʃ/?	/s/ or /ʃ/?
-ti-	**-ci-**	**-ssi-, -ssu-**
na**ti**onal debt	so**ci**al event	I a**ssu**re you
essen**ti**al details	spe**ci**al project	blood pre**ssu**re
next genera**ti**on	effi**ci**ent way	serious i**ssu**es
ra**ti**o of 7:1	suspi**ci**ous person	severe rece**ssi**on

✔ **Complete the Rule:** The *-ti-, -ci-, -ssi-,* and *-ssu-* in suffixes or word endings are additional spellings for the /   / sound as in _____.

Rule 3-2

The /tʃ/ sound is commonly spelled **ch** *as in* **ch**oose.

Listen to the italicized letters in the phrases. Circle the sound you hear. Do you hear . . .

/t/ or /tʃ/?

-tu-

serious si**tu**ation

the near fu**tu**re

na**tu**ral ingredients

21st cen**tu**ry

✔ **Complete the Rule:** The *-tu-* in suffixes and word endings is another spelling for the /   / sound as in _____.

More Sound/Spelling Notes for /tʃ/ as in **ch**oose: (1) The *ch* in these words sounds like /ʃ/ as in **sh**oe: *machine, chef, champagne, Chicago,* and *Michigan;* (2) The *ch* in these words sounds like /k/ as in *key: architecture, chaos, chemical, chronic, cholera, stomachache, orchestra,* and *chlorine;* (3) When *-n-* precedes *-ti-* (at**ten**ti**on, presiden**ti**al, creden**ti**als), the *-ti-* can be pronounced /ʃ/ as in **sh**oe or /tʃ/ as in **ch**oose.

Rule 3-3

*The /ʒ/ as in mea**su**re never occurs at the beginnings of words.*

Listen to the italicized letters. Circle the sound you hear in each column. Do you hear . . .

/z/, /ʃ/, or /ʒ/?	/z/, /ʃ/, or /ʒ/?
-si-	**-su-**
head-on colli**si**on	precise mea**su**rement
minor revi**si**on	expo**su**re to the sun
divi**si**on of power	lei**su**re-time activities
central A**si**a	ca**su**al clothing

✔ **Complete the Rule:** The *-si-* and *-su-* in suffixes are common spellings for the / / sound as in _____ . (*Pronunciation Hint: /ʒ/ = /ʃ/ + voicing.**)

Rule 3-4

*The /dʒ/ sound is commonly spelled **j** (job) and **g** (general).*

Listen to the italicized letters. Circle the sound that you hear. Do you hear . . .

/d/ or /dʒ/?

-du-

indivi**du**al rights

e**du**cated guess

recent gra**du**ate

new proce**du**res

✔ **Complete the Rule:** The *-du-* in the middle of words is another spelling for the / / sound as in _____ . (*Pronunciation Hint: /dʒ/ = /tʃ/ + voicing.*)

*voicing = vocal cord vibration

A HELPFUL HINT

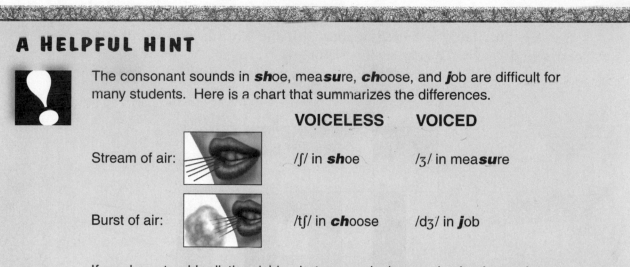

The consonant sounds in **sh**oe, mea**su**re, **ch**oose, and **j**ob are difficult for many students. Here is a chart that summarizes the differences.

	VOICELESS	VOICED
Stream of air:	/ʃ/ in **sh**oe	/ʒ/ in mea**su**re
Burst of air:	/tʃ/ in **ch**oose	/dʒ/ in **j**ob

If you have trouble distinguishing between voiceless and voiced sounds, try covering your ears with your hands. This emphasizes low frequencies and causes voiced consonants to sound especially loud.

Exercise 1

With a partner, write the phrases in the correct columns below.

nego**ti**ate a contract	mu**tu**al friend
very profe**ssi**onal	long divi**si**on
my plea**su**re	resche**du**le the meeting
so**ci**al event	depar**tu**re time
wedding ri**tu**al	gra**du**al improvement
poor vi**si**on	resi**du**al amount

Column 1	Column 2	Column 3	Column 4
/ʃ/ as in **sh**oe	/tʃ/ as in **ch**oose	/ʒ/ as in mea**su**re	/dʒ/ as in **j**ob
Negotiate	mutual	vision	gradual
Professional	departure	division	residual
Social	ritual	Pleasure	reschedule

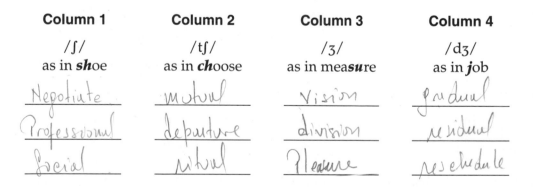

Repeat each list of phrases after your teacher or the speaker on tape.

Exercise 2

With a partner, add the endings to the words and write the new words in the crossword puzzle. Change spellings if necessary.

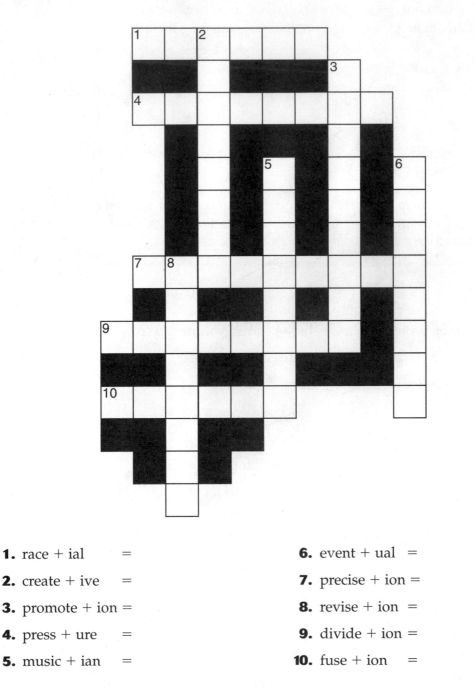

1. race + ial   =

2. create + ive   =

3. promote + ion =

4. press + ure   =

5. music + ian   =

6. event + ual =

7. precise + ion =

8. revise + ion =

9. divide + ion =

10. fuse + ion   =

Practice saying the base words and the new words with your teacher or the speaker on tape. Check the most difficult words and practice them with your class.

SOMETHING TO THINK ABOUT

In this class, you will be asked to monitor or listen carefully to the following:

- **A classmate's pronunciation while she or he is speaking.** If you hear a problem, don't interrupt. Note the problem and call it to your classmate's attention after she or he finishes speaking. Give your classmate the opportunity to correct the error. Remember that pronunciation is a sensitive area for many learners.

- **Your pronunciation while you are speaking.** If you hear a problem while you are speaking, correct it if the situation allows. If not, just note the problem and go on.

- **Your pronunciation on audiotape or videotape.** If you hear a problem on tape, stop the recorder. Rewind and listen again. Then try to correct the pronunciation yourself.

When monitoring, focus on one or two pronunciation points at a time. Listen for clear, as well as unclear, pronunciations. Monitoring is difficult at first but gets easier with practice. As your peer monitoring gets better, your self-monitoring will improve.

Exercise 3

In circles of three or four, do a round-robin reading of "American Government" at the beginning of the chapter. In a round-robin reading, each student takes turns reading a sentence. Repeat the reading by having a different student in the group start the passage.

Monitor your classmates' pronunciation of the italicized spellings.

Rule 3-5

Listen to the *qu* spelling pattern. Circle the sound(s) that you hear. Do you hear . . .

/k/ or /kw/?

qu- and ***-qu-***

qualified applicant   KW

complicated e***qu***ation   K

outdated e***qu***ipment   KW

proper se***qu***ence   K

☑ **Complete the Rule:** The *-qu-* and *qu-* spellings are pronounced like the two sounds /   /. (*Pronunciation Hint:* Round the lips for /w/ before you release the /k/ sound.)

Rule 3-6

Listen to the *x* and *cc* spelling patterns. Do you hear one or two sounds? Circle the sound(s) you hear. Do you hear . . .

/s/ or /ks/?	/s/ or /ks/?
-x-	**-cc-** *(before i and e)*
ex*cept* the teacher *ks*	a**cc**ept the consequences *kss*
ex*cuse* me *s*	su**cc**eed in business *s*
valuable ex*perience* *s*	serious a**cc**ident *ks*
an ex*treme* position *s*	a**cc**ess to the Internet *ks*

✔ **Complete the Rule:** The *-x-* and *-cc-* spellings are usually pronounced like the TWO sounds /   /.

Exercise 4

Repeat the sentences below after your teacher or the speaker on tape or practice with a partner, using the following procedure:

Example: Starter Phrase   *Completion Phrases*

That company spe**ci**alizes in . . .   office furni**tu**re.

                                             ero**si**on control.

                                             pa**ti**ent safety.

Step 1: Student 2 closes the book. Student 1 gives student 2 the starter phrase to memorize: *"That company specializes in . . ."*

Step 2: Student 1 gives student 2 the first completion phrase—*office furniture.* Student 2 says the whole sentence: *"That company specializes in office furniture."*

Step 3: Student 1 gives student 2 the next completion phrase—*erosion control.* Student 2 says the same starter phrase with the next completion phrase: *"That company specializes in erosion control."* And so on . . .

Starter Phrases   *Completion Phrases*

1. When is the next . . .   quiz?

                                     quarterly report?

                                     qualifying exam?

                                     quality control meeting?

Note: The *-x-* in *example, exact, executive,* and *examine* is pronounced as a voiced /gz/.

2. What is the situation with . . .

the joint venture?

our natural resources?

the featured speaker?

our future earnings?

(Switch Roles.)

3. Those were good . . .

decisions.

revisions.

audiovisuals.

measurements.

4. When did they schedule . . .

graduation?

your procedure?

the graduate student meeting?

individual conferences?

Rules and Practices 2:
Final Consonant Sounds and Spellings

Final consonants make speech clear, yet they are especially troublesome. Some students omit final consonants; they might say *"bo- answer-"* for *"bo**th** answer**s**."* Other students confuse final voiceless and voiced consonants; they might say *"Half a good day!"* for *"Have a good day!"*

Final consonant sounds are either voiceless (no vocal cord vibration) or voiced (vocal cord vibration):

	Consonant Pair Sounds	Other Consonant Sounds
Voiceless	p t k f θ s ʃ tʃ	h
Voiced	b d g v ð z ʒ dʒ	m n ŋ l r w y

See Appendix B for a complete overview of voiceless and voiced consonants.

Sometimes spelling indicates whether a final consonant is voiced or voiceless (*nee**d*** and *nea**t***). Sometimes it does not (*close* as a verb /kloʷz/ and *close* as an adjective /kloʷs/). These final consonant guidelines will help make your speech clearer.

Rule 3-7

Listen to the final voiceless and voiced consonant sounds. Can you hear a difference?

VOICELESS	VOICED
safe	save
safe neighborhoods	save neighborhoods
white	wide
a white door	a wide door
price	prize
the best price	the best prize
lap	lab
lap computer	lab computer

Differences between final voiceless and voiced consonants are hard to hear. Maybe you hear differences in the preceding vowels. In which column do the vowels sound longer?

☑ **Complete the Rule:** Vowels sound longer before final __voiced__ consonants.

Rule 3-8

The following word pairs are spelled the same but pronounced differently. What is the difference in pronunciation?

NOUNS/ ADJECTIVES	VERBS
use	use
close	close
excuse	excuse
abuse	abuse

In which column are the vowels longer? In which column are the final consonants voiced?

☑ **Complete the Rule:** In the pairs above, final consonants are __voiceless__ in nouns/adjectives and __voiced__ in verbs.

Exercise 5

Repeat the phrases after the speaker on tape or practice with your teacher. If your teacher says a phrase from the first column (*"half a cookie"*), say the pair phrase from the second column (*"have a cookie"*), and viceversa. Remember to l-e-n-g-t-h-e-n the vowels in the verb forms. Link the final consonant with the next word in each phrase.

NOUN/ ADJECTIVE FORMS	VERB FORMS
1. half a cookie	have a cookie
2. belief in yourself	believe in yourself
3. safe money	save money
4. advice about courses	advise about courses
5. relief from pain	relieve from pain
6. loose change	lose change
7. use in the kitchen	use in the kitchen
8. close windows	close windows
9. house guests	house guests
10. excuse from class	excuse from class

Exercise 6

Listen carefully as your teacher or the speaker on tape says each sentence twice. Did you hear the italicized word the first time (1) or the second time (2)? Circle 1 or 2.

Example: 1 (2) *That's a **wide** door.*

1.	1	2	Have a **safe** trip.
2.	1	2	I **need** two pounds of fish.
3.	1	2	I can't **believe** it.
4.	1	2	Can you **prove** it?
5.	1	2	**Leave** the key at the desk.
6.	1	2	He got a **cake** for the party.
7.	1	2	Did you **close** the account?
8.	1	2	Where's the first-aid **kit?**
9.	1	2	Would you **excuse** me.
10.	1	2	I'll **have** a cup of coffee.

Check your answers with your teacher. With a partner, take turns saying the above sentences. Monitor your partner.

A HELPFUL HINT

How do you address women in the United States?

Miss = /mɪs/, for unmarried women

Ms. = /mɪz/, for married or unmarried women

Missus (Mrs.) = /mɪsəz/, for married women

These titles are used before a woman's last or family name. Many women prefer the general title Ms. to Miss or Mrs. because Ms. can be used without regard to marital status. Ms. is also the correct title for a married woman who keeps her own name after marriage.

Exercise 7

Listen to your teacher or the speaker on tape say titles and names. Check *Married* if you hear Mrs., *Single* if you hear Miss, and *Don't Know* if you hear Ms. Remember that Ms., with the final voiced /z/, sounds almost twice as long as Miss, with the final voiceless /s/.

Mrs. – Married	Miss – Single	Ms. – Don't Know
Example:		✔
1.	√ √	
2.	√	
3.	√	
4.		√
5.	√	
6.	√	
7.		√

Check your answers with your teacher.

Communicative Practice: Evacuate!

Imagine that you are a member of a family living in a coastal area about to be struck by a hurricane. Your neighborhood must be evacuated to an elementary school that is inland. Families have only 15 minutes to gather items from their homes. Each family includes a grandfather, a wife, a husband, a seven-year-old son, and an eight-month-old daughter.

Listed on page 30 are some items you might want to take with you to the shelter. Follow these steps and rank the 10 items you would take.

Step 1: Preview Pronunciation

Practice the sound/spelling patterns in useful words and phrases:

We have to make a deci**si**on . . .

That's not essen**ti**al . . .

We nee**d**/don't nee**d** . . .

I think/don't think *we'd* use . . .

Preview the sound/spelling patterns in words from the evacuation list:

medica**ti**on, pre**ssu**re, finan**ci**al, televi**si**on, e**x**tra, te**x**tbooks, and bo**x**.

Preview the final consonants in words from the evacuation list. Remember to lengthen vowels before final voiced consonants: ca**t**, foo**d**, fi**v**e, ai**d**, soa**p**, and ki**t**.

Step 2: Rank Items Individually

Take five minutes and individually rank the 10 most important items (1 = most essential; 2 = next most essential; and so on). Give reasons for your choices.

Step 3: Achieve Consensus

In the remaining 10 minutes, share your individual rankings in groups of five students. Try to reach agreement as a "family" about what to take. Report your top choices and reasons to the class.

Evacuation List*	Personal Ranking	Reason	Family Ranking	Reason
Ca**t**				
Cat foo**d**				
Flashlight				
Grandfather's blood pre**ssu**re medica**ti**on				
E**x**tra change of clothe**s**				
Blankets				
Battery-powered televi**si**on				
Baby foo**d**				
Important finan**ci**al documents				
Family photographs				
Diapers				
Candles				
Canned foo**d**				
Games/books for recrea**ti**on				
Cosmetics				
Fi**v**e-gallon water container				
School te**x**tbooks				
Soa**p** and towels				
Bo**x** of matches				
First-ai**d** ki**t**				

*Adapted from Connie L. Shoemaker and F. Floyd Shoemaker, *Interactive Techniques for the ESL Classroom* (New York: Newbury House Publishers, 1991), pp. 128–129. Used with permission.

Extend Your Skills . . . to Reporting an Emergency

When calling to report an emergency, clear communication is important. In this pair practice, one student is a caller who reports an accident, a fire, wind damage, or other emergency over a bad telephone connection. The other student is a dispatcher who receives the call and records the information. The caller and the dispatcher should sit back-to-back.

Caller: Decide on an emergency situation. Call 911 and state that you are reporting an emergency. Describe the emergency and give your name and address. Remember that the telephone connection is bad, so pronounce all sounds slowly and carefully, especially final consonants in location names and numbers.

Dispatcher: Record the information so that you can dispatch (send) emergency personnel to the location. Ask the caller to repeat any information that is not clear. Tell the caller that help will arrive in a few minutes.

A HELPFUL HINT

Unlearning old habits of speaking and learning new ones is difficult and sometimes tedious. These strategies will help develop your awareness of consonant sounds and make your out-of-class practice more effective.

1. **Focus on the feel** of the new sounds. Practice silently and s-l-o-w-l-y. Mouth the beginning, middle, and end of words. Then say the words out loud.

2. **Focus on the sound** of the new pattern. Practice with your eyes closed.

3. **Focus on the look** of the new sounds. Practice in front of a mirror. Imitate the facial positions and mouth movements of American English speakers. Clear English pronunciation requires active use of the mouth, lips, and jaw.

Remember to keep a list of difficult words you want to learn. Review them frequently, using these strategies. Practice the words in typical phrases and sentences you would say in real situations. Imagine that you are an actor rehearsing before you go onstage.

PRIME-TIME PRACTICE

Prime-time practice is oral homework, usually completed during the prime-time hours of 7:00 P.M. and 11:00 P.M.

See the Oral Review on the next page. Read it silently for meaning. Then read it out loud. Write the five most difficult words or phrases:

1. _____

2. _____

3. _____

4. _____

5. _____

Practice the words/phrases, using the strategies in A Helpful Hint above. Which of the three strategies seemed the most helpful? _____

Oral Review: Sound and Spelling Patterns

Name: _____ Date: _____

Directions: You are a member of a nonprofit group that educates the public about the environment. A local radio station has donated broadcast time to your organization. You have been selected to tape the first announcement in a series of short public-service broadcasts. Practice and then record the following announcement. Submit the cassette to your teacher.

Public-Service Announcement

Good evening, everyone.

Earth Day 1990 called worldwide **attention** to the **future** of our environment. Many people **believe** that our planet faces serious threats and that we **need** to take immediate steps to **save** it. Here are some of the most serious environmental problems and some things **individuals** can do to improve the **situation.**

Scientists are **expressing** concern about damage to the ozone layer caused by human-made gases escaping into the atmosphere. **Erosion** of the ozone layer has already resulted in increased rates of skin cancer from **exposure** to harmful rays of the sun. What can we do? Use air **conditioners** sparingly. Avoid using plastic foam products like Styrofoam cups. Pay **attention** to labels on aerosol spray cans because they may contain ozone-depleting **chemicals.**

Scientists are also **expressing** concern about the greenhouse effect, the **gradual** warming of the earth from the buildup of gases like carbon **dioxide.** The increase in **temperatures** would cause **glaciers** to melt and sea levels to rise. Huge shifts would also occur in rainfall and **agricultural** patterns. What can we do? Buy energy-**efficient** appliances and fuel-**efficient** cars. Get annual auto **emission inspections.** Set thermostats in your homes to lower **temperatures.**

The third problem is garbage overload and the **contamination** of ground-water. **Individuals** can address this **issue** by recycling newspapers, cans, glass, and plastics. Local governments can increase fines for industrial **pollution** and restrict **commercial** development near streams and rivers.

This is the first in our series of **special** announcements called "What on Earth Can We Do?" Help us with **future** broadcasts by telling us what you think the most pressing environmental **issues** are and what ordinary citizens like you are doing to **ensure** environmental **quality** for the next **generation.** Call 555-2000 and leave a 90-second message on our answering **machine.**

Listen to your tape before you submit it. Monitor your pronunciation of all italicized words. Make corrections at the end of your tape by repeating any sentences with incorrect words or phrases.

Syllables and Word Endings

W ords in English have one or more syllables, or beats. Listen to the words below. How many beats do you hear in each word?

act	active	actively	activity
vent	invent	invented	inventory

Now say the words with your teacher and tap the syllables or beats on your desk.

tap	*tap tap*	*tap tap tap*	*tap tap tap tap*
act	ac tive	ac tive ly	ac tiv i ty
vent	in vent	in vent ed	in ven tor y

Learners of English might drop syllables from words or add extra syllables. Dropping and adding syllables makes words difficult to understand. In this chapter, you will become more aware of the importance of syllables and word endings.

Listen!

Listening Activity 1

Listen to your teacher or the speaker on tape say the phrase from each pair. Check the one you hear.

Examples: _____ start the car   __✔__ started the car

__✔__ slight accent   _____ slight accident

1. _____ just find the answer	_____ justified the answer
2. _____ canned a salmon	_____ Canada salmon
3. _____ planned a garden	_____ planted a garden
4. _____ turned around	_____ turn it around
5. _____ X-rayed	_____ X-rated
6. _____ Miss Smith	_____ Mrs. Smith
7. _____ change the date	_____ change the data
8. _____ popular present	_____ popular president
9. _____ enormous scar	_____ enormous cigar
10. _____ gracious hosts	_____ gracious hostess

Check your answers with your teacher.

Listen to your teacher or the speaker on tape say *both* phrases in each pair. What is the difference between the phrases in each set?

Listening Activity 2

Close your book and listen to a short passage about color preference. The speaker will habitually omit an important feature of English pronunciation and grammar. What is missing?*

How did this passage sound *without -s* endings? The absence of final *-s* might not interfere with understanding, but it might be distracting and interfere with the listener's ability to concentrate on what is being said.

Now listen to the speaker read the passage with -s endings. Fill in the blanks with the words you hear. Notice how frequently -s endings occur.

Color Preference‡

For many _____years_____, _____scientists_____ have been studying the _____factors_____ that influence human preference in _____colors_____. Although the _____results_____ are inconclusive, the _____conclusions_____ have been used to make _____decisions_____ about _____colors_____ used in decorating and in the packaging of consumer _____goods_____.

One factor that _____influences_____ human preference in _____colors_____ is age. _____babies_____ are attracted to bright, warm _____colors_____, such as yellow and red. _____Adults_____, in contrast, prefer cool _____colors_____, such as blue and green.

In addition, where people live _____affects_____ color preference. Often a _____person's_____ home _____reflects_____ a color break from the outside environment. The brown scenery in the Southwest _____offers_____ little color, so _____houses_____ there have pink, orange, and other vibrant _____colors_____. In industrial _____cities_____ of the North, white _____curtains_____ are preferred despite the industrial smoke and soot.

*ANSWER: Did you notice that all of the -s endings on nouns and verbs were missing?

‡ Information adapted from "The Blueing of America," Time, July 18, 1983, p. 62; Leslie Kane, "The Power of Color," Health, July 1982, p. 37; Birren Faber, *Color and Human Response* (John Wiley and Sons, 1997).

Finally, many _researches_ believe that personality _Affect_ color choice. A person who _likes_ red is athletic and extroverted. Someone who _prefers_ orange is friendly; a person who _likes_ pink is feminine and charming; a person who _loves_ blue may be intellectual and conservative; and a person who _likes_ purple is aristocratic and artistic.

Dictate to your teacher the words you wrote in the blanks.

Rules and Practices 1: Syllables and -s Endings

Rule 4-1

We pronounce -s endings on simple present tense verbs, plural nouns, and possessive nouns in three ways.

Listen and write what the -s ending sounds like in each group:

1. teach/teach**es**	office/offic**es**	George/George's	= _əz_ / _ɪz_
2. pay/pay**s**	read/read**s**	Laura/Laura's	= _z_
3. fit/fit**s**	work/work**s**	Mark/Mark's	= _s_

Compare your answers with these rules:

✔ **1.** In words that end in the hissing, sibilant sounds /s/, /z/, /ʃ/, /ʒ/, /tʃ/, and /dʒ/, like words in group 1, add the *syllable* /əz/ or /ɪz/.

✔ **2.** In words ending in a voiced sound, like words in group 2, add the *sound* /z/ as in *zoo*.

✔ **3.** In words ending in a voiceless sound, like words in group 3, add the *sound* /s/ as in *so*.

Drawing by Rivi; © 1998 The New Yorker Magazine, Inc.
Reprinted by permission.

Exercise 1

Part A: Say the word pairs below with your teacher or the speaker on tape. Count the syllables in each pair.

Final /əz/ Syllable	*Final /z/ Sound*	*Final /s/ Sound*
finish/finishes (2/3)	allow/allows (2/2)	limit/limits (2/2)
chance/chances (/)	skill/skills (/)	asset/assets (/)
cause/causes (/)	copy/copies (/)	sock/socks (/)

Part B: Add an -s ending to each word below and say it. Write each word in the correct column.

Word	Add a Syllable	Add a Sound
1. course	*courses*	
2. grade		*grades*
3. speech	speeches	
4. estimate		estimates
5. erase	erases	
6. plan		plans
7. laugh*		laughs
8. result		results

Check your answers with your teacher.

Exercise 2

Part A: Say the word pairs with the speaker on tape or work with a partner as follows: If one student says a word from column A, the other student says the pair word from column B and vice versa.

Example: If one student says *"chances,"* the other student says *"chance."*

A	B	A	B
chance	chances	count	county
page	pages	eight	eighty
hosts	hostess	date	data
piece	pieces	quote	quota
folks	focus	claps	collapse
notice	notices	prayed	parade
runway	runaway	state	estate

*The gh spelling at the ends of words (laugh, enough, tough) is usually pronounced as a voiceless /f/.

Part B: Say the statements and responses with the speakers on tape or practice with a partner as follows: Student 1 covers the responses and says statement a or b. Student 2 covers the statements and gives the correct response. Switch roles and repeat.

STATEMENTS (STUDENT 1)	RESPONSES (STUDENT 2)
1. a. She had a big *part*.	She did most of the research.
b. She had a big *party*.	She invited sixty people.
2. a. I helped the *hosts*.	They needed it.
b. I helped the *hostess*.	She needed it.
3. a. He *let* me borrow his car.	Last week.
b. She *lets* me borrow her car.	Regularly.
4. a. Do you have the *date?*	It's on my calendar.
b. Do you have the *data?*	It's still being processed.
5. a. He missed his *chance* to make up the test.	And he had only one.
b. He missed his *chances* to make up the test.	And he had three!
6. a. The airline found your *suitcase*.	Where was it?
b. The airline found your *suitcases*.	Where were they?
7. a. Her name is *Miss* Smith.	She's single?
b. Her name is *Mrs*. Smith.	She's married?
8. a. What do I owe you for the *ticket?*	It was $15.00.
b. What do I owe you for the *tickets?*	They were $60.00.
9. a. He lost his *folks*.	In the airport.
b. He lost his *focus*.	On the project.
10. a. I got an *eight* dollar fine.	Not bad!
b. I got an *eighty* dollar fine.	Too bad!

Exercise 3

Part A: In the box below, circle the count nouns with singular and plural forms like *key/keys* and *bus/buses*. Noncount nouns like *homework* and *water* are neither singular nor plural. Some nouns like *time* can be count or noncount, depending on the context. Check your answers with your teacher.

Practice the count nouns in both the singular and the plural with the speaker on tape or with your teacher.

advantage	time	method	page
system	feedback	procedure	week
graph	possibility	input	approach
customer	consequence	case	increase
expense	experience	merchandise	luggage
note	mail	homework	desk
research	difference	evidence	box

Part B: In this pair practice, Student 1 says the simple form of one of the words above. Student 2 substitutes the word into one of the common phrases below, adding -s if necessary.

Examples: Student 1 says "merchandise."
      Student 2 says "a little merchandise."
        (or)
      Student 1 says "box."
      Student 2 says "a few boxes."

COUNT NOUNS	**NONCOUNT NOUNS**
not many _____	not much _____
a few _____	a little _____
a lot of _____	a lot of _____

Exercise 4

Proverbs are short, popular sayings. As timeless truths, proverbs are usually expressed in the present tense.

Underline the verbs below. Say the proverbs with the speaker on tape or with a partner. Monitor the -s endings on the verbs.

1. Absence makes the heart grow fonder.

2. The devil dances in an empty pocket.

3. The early bird catches the worm.

4. One good turn deserves another.

5. All work and no play makes Jack a dull boy.

6. All that glitters is not gold.

7. An apple a day keeps the doctor away.

8. Time flies when you are having fun.

9. Practice makes perfect.

10. The last straw breaks the camel's back.

Translate two proverbs from your language. Underline any verbs that end with -s. Share your proverbs with your class.

11. _____

12. _____

A HELPFUL HINT

Words that end in two consonant sounds (e.g., te**st** and dire**ct**) might be difficult for you to pronounce. Adding a final -s increases the difficulty. Here are some ways that native speakers simplify these kinds of consonant sequences.

1. Many common words end in -ct (fa**ct**), -pt (conce**pt**), and -nd (frie**nd**). When an -s is added, native speakers usually drop the -t or -d: fac̸ts, conce̸pts, frie̸nds.

2. When -s is added to words that end in -st (li**st**) and -sk (a**sk**), native speakers tend to drop the -t (gues̸ts) or -k (as̸ks) and to lengthen the /s/.

Exercise 5

Repeat these words and phrases after your teacher or the speaker on tape. Make a smooth transition from the final -s to the next word in each phrase.

ct+s	*pt+s*	*nd+s*
fact/fac̸ts (sounds like *fax*)	adapt/adap̸ts	send/sen̸ds
fac̸ts in the case	adap̸ts well	sen̸ds messages
act/ac̸ts (sounds like *ax*)	concept/concep̸ts	lend/len̸ds
ac̸ts like he's mad	concep̸ts in the text	len̸ds money
direct/direc̸ts	corrupt/corrup̸ts	friend/frien̸ds
direc̸ts traffic	corrup̸ts the results	frien̸ds and family

These consonant sequences may also occur across word boundaries. Repeat these examples:

1. Voters will elec̸t city officials.
2. Deduc̸t seven dollars from the total.
3. They should accep̸t some of the blame.
4. Sen̸d some more money.

Exercise 6

Listen to the contrast between careful pronunciation and normal, rapid speech. The symbol (:) signals length.

1. Put the (desks/des:s) in the storage room.
2. I got the (lists/lis:s) of names.
3. She (asks/as:s) too many questions.
4. Have the (guests/gues:s) left?
5. I passed all of my (tests/tes:s) and quizzes.

Repeat each group of words below after your teacher or the speaker on tape.

1. guess   guest   guest is   guests or gues:s
2. Tess   test   test is   tests or tes:s
3. chess   chest   chest is   chests or ches:s

The *st+s* sequences may also occur across word boundaries. Repeat these examples.

1. Mos*t* stores open at 10:00.
2. She was the las*t* student to finish.
3. What's the bes*t* song on the tape?

Communicative Practice 1: Stockroom Inventory*

Practice plural nouns as you and your partner do a stockroom inventory for a college bookstore. The Stockroom Order Form on page 41 is missing information. Your task is to complete the form and then telephone the order to the stockroom manager.

Student 1 will work from Stock List A on page 137, and Student 2 will use Stock List B on page 138. Only part of the information you need is on each stock list, so you need to share your data to complete the order form. Sit back-to-back and do not look at your partner's stock list.

Tape-record your completed order to the stockroom manager. Listen to the tape and monitor your *-s* endings.

*Courtesy of David Miller, Instructor, Language Institute, Georgia Institute of Technology, Atlanta, Georgia.

STOCKROOM ORDER FORM	DATE: _____
Items to be ordered:	**Quantity:**
Computer monitors	
Computer keyboards	
Desktop computer systems	
Business software packages	
TOEFL review books	
Art brushes	
T-shirts	
Scientific calculators	
Pairs of sunglasses	
Pencil cases	
Alarm clocks	

Rules and Practices 2:
Syllables and *-ed* Endings

Rule 4-2

We pronounce the **-ed** *ending on regular verbs in three ways.*

Listen and write down what the *-ed* sounds like in the sentences below.

1. I wait for the bus.
I wait**ed** for the bus.　　= _____

2. The labs close at eight.
The labs clos**ed** at eight. = _____

3. They work hard.
They work**ed** hard.　　= _____

Compare your answers with these rules.

☑　**1.** In verbs that end in /t/ or /d/, like wai**t**, the *-ed* is spoken as the extra *syllable* /əd/ or /ɪd/.

☑　**2.** In verbs that end in voiced sounds, like the verb clo**s**e, the *-ed* sounds like the voiced *sound* /d/ as in *dime*.

☑　**3.** In verbs that end in voiceless sounds, like wor**k**, the *-ed* sounds like the voiceless *sound* /t/ as in *time*.

Note: The *-ed* adjectives and the *-edly* adverbs add the syllable /əd/.
Examples: a wicked person　　　　(wicked = 2 syllables)
　　　　a naked baby　　　　　(naked = 2 syllables)
　　　　supposedly accurate records　(supposedly = 4 syllables)

Exercise 7

Part A: Say the verb pairs below with your teacher or the speaker on tape. Write the number of syllables in each word pair.

Final /əd/	*Final /d/*	*Final /t/*
construct/constructed (2/3)	install/installed (2/2)	talk/talked (1/1)
decide/decided (/)	save/saved (/)	laugh/laughed (/)
graduate/graduated (/)	delay/delayed (/)	process/processed (/)

Part B: Add *-ed* to the following verbs and say them. Did you add the syllable /əd/ or the sound /d/ or /t/? Write the words in the correct column below.

Verb	Add a Syllable	Add a Sound
1. turn		*turned*
2. repeat	*repeated*	
3. crash		
4. provide		
5. work		
6. refuse		
7. evaluate		
8. plan		

Check your answers with your teacher.

A HELPFUL HINT

Your pronunciation of the past tense **-ed** will sound more natural if you link it with the next word in the verb phrase.

1. Notice what happens when the word after the past tense ending begins with a vowel.

stressed out	(sounds like *stress-dout*)
cooked it	(sounds like *cook-dit*)

2. Notice what happens when the past tense ending is the same as or similar to the first sound in the next word.

planned to go	(sounds like *plan to go*)
listened to	(sounds like *listen to*)
fixed the VCR	(sounds like *fix the VCR*)

Even though you see white space between words on the page, do not separate the verb from the next word in the phrase.

Exercise 8

Practice past tense endings and link them with the next word in each verb phrase. After you say each sentence, listen to your teacher or the speaker on tape say the same sentence. Was yours correct?

1. He filled out the application.

2. The meeting's been called off.

3. I checked in this morning.

4. She's already checked out.

5. Carlos majored in economics.

6. The teacher has already handed our papers back.

7. He pointed out all of my mistakes.

8. That model will be gradually phased out.

9. I have already turned down three offers.

10. I've looked over your résumé.

Which past tense form above was difficult to hear? Why?

Communicative Practice 2: Revealing Your Past

In small groups of four or five, use the verbs in the box below to write three statements about your past education, employment, or free-time activities. Two statements should be true, and one should be false.

Read your statements to the group. Members of the group should write the statement they think is false and then compare guesses.

Preview the pronunciation of key past tense verbs that might be useful in a job interview.

KEY PAST TENSE VERBS			
started	attended	participated in	increased
completed	planned	worked	conducted
graduated	studied	volunteered	coordinated
obtained	evaluated	served	improved
helped	coached	played	researched
managed	organized	supervised	owned

Statement 1: _____

Statement 2: _____

Statement 3: _____

PRIME-TIME PRACTICE

Past Tense Narrative

A short narrative that teaches a lesson or moral is called a *fable*. Fables are still told today and are as popular as they were during Aesop's time in ancient Greece. In this fable, you will practice *-ed* endings.

Step 1: Read the fable silently. Underline every past tense *-ed* verb and link (‿) it to the next word in the same phrase.

Step 2: Record yourself reading the fable.

Step 3: Listen to the recording and monitor verbs with *-ed* endings. Rerecord any verb phrases you are not satisfied with. Give the tape to your teacher for feedback.

The Man with Two Wives

In the days when men were allowed to have many wives, a middle-aged man had one young wife and one old one. Each loved him very much and desired to see him like herself. Now the man's hair was turning gray, which the young woman did not like because it made him look too old to be her husband. So every night she combed his hair and picked out the white strands. The elder wife saw her husband growing old with great pleasure, for she didn't like to be mistaken for his mother. So every morning she arranged his hair and picked out as many black strands as she could. The consequence was the man soon found himself entirely bald.

Moral: Yield to all, and you will soon have nothing to yield.

Extend Your Skills . . . to Descriptions of Graphs

Explaining graphs is a useful academic/business skill. In this activity, you will practice -s endings as you explain information presented in graph form.

Step 1: Preview the five parts of your explanation and practice useful phrases.

PART	-s FORMS IN USEFUL PHRASES
a. Subject of the Graph	This graph shows . . . This graph illustrates . . .
b. Components of the Graph	The x (horizontal) axis represents . . . The y (vertical) axis indicates . . .
c. Patterns	This graph demonstrates . . . One of the trends is . . . As _____ increases, . . . As _____ decreases, . . .
d. Example	For example, . . . For instance, . . .
e. Predictions or Implications	If this pattern (trend) continues . . . If this trend holds . . . One of the conclusions is . . . One of the implications is . . .

Note: When speaking of trends, increases, or decreases, terms like *slight(ly)*, *gradual(ly)*, *sharp(ly)*, *dramatic(ally)*, and *significant(ly)* may be useful.

Step 2: Choose a graph from the following pages or find one of interest in a magazine or text. Spend five minutes outlining a short explanation. Present the explanation to the class or to a small group. (Use notes but do not read your explanation.) Be prepared to answer questions. Record your explanation on an audiocassette.

Step 3: After class, listen to your tape and evaluate your presentation on the "Explaining a Graph/Self-Evaluation Form." Submit the form to your teacher.

Explaining A Graph/Self-Evaluation Form*

Name: _____ Date: _____

Part I. Listen to the tape. Write down every noun and verb with an -s ending.

Part II. Assign 1 point for each part of the explanation below. You might need to listen to the tape several times.

  A. Organization   1 point each

      1. Subject clearly stated   _____

      2. Each component identified   _____

      3. Patterns/trends identified   _____

      4. One example given   _____

      5. End clearly indicated   _____

                            (Part A) _____ × 10 = _____

  B. Pronunciation   1 point each

      1. Adequate volume   _____

      2. Good speed   _____

      3. Clear key words   _____

      4. Final -s about 75% correct   _____

      5. Good overall clarity   _____

                            (Part B) _____ × 10 = _____

                        TOTAL (Part A + B) = _____%

Comments:

_____

_____

_____

_____

Note: You may also use this form to evaluate a peer presentation or tape.

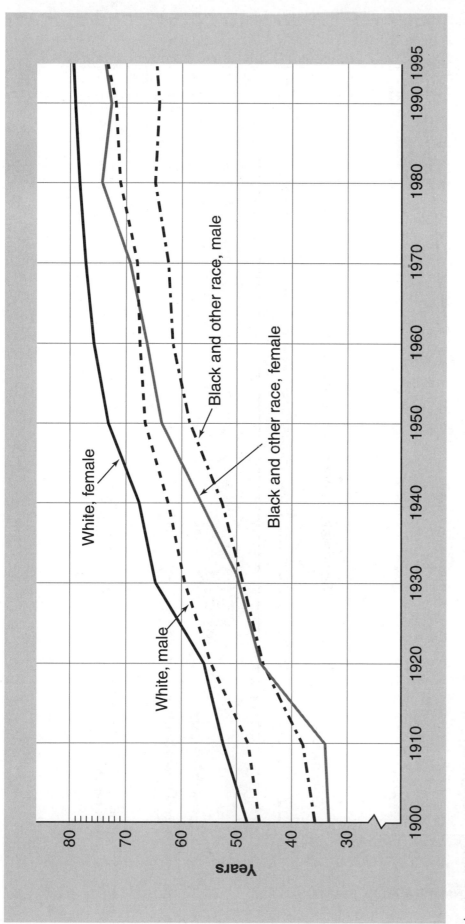

▲ Life Expectancy at Birth by gender: United States, 1900—95.

Sources: U.S. Department of Health, Education and Welfare, Public Health Service, National Center for Health Statistics, *Vital Statistics of the United States 1973*, Vol. 2, part A, section 5, and Centers for Disease Control, *Monthly Vital Statistics Report*, Vol 45, No. 11(S)2, June 12, 1997, p. 19.

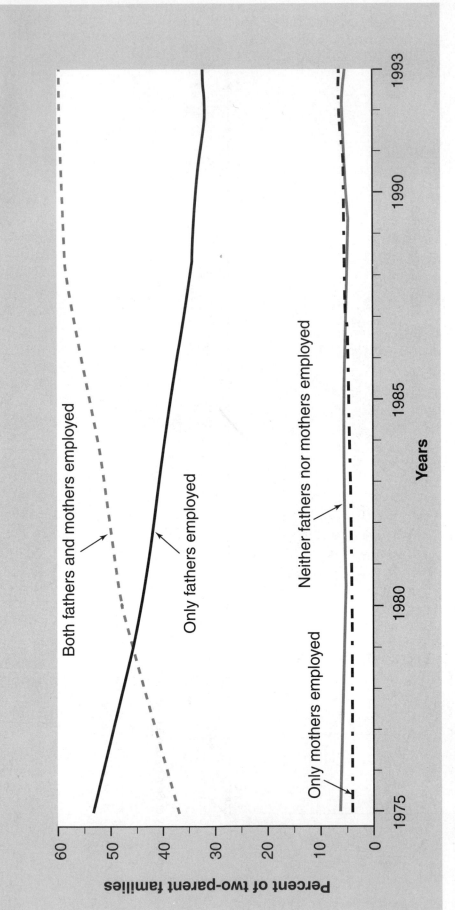

▲ Employment Status of Married Couples with Children (under 18 years), 1975–1993.

Source: U.S. Department of Education, *Trends in the Well-Being of American Youth, Youth Indicators 1996*, Indicator 18.

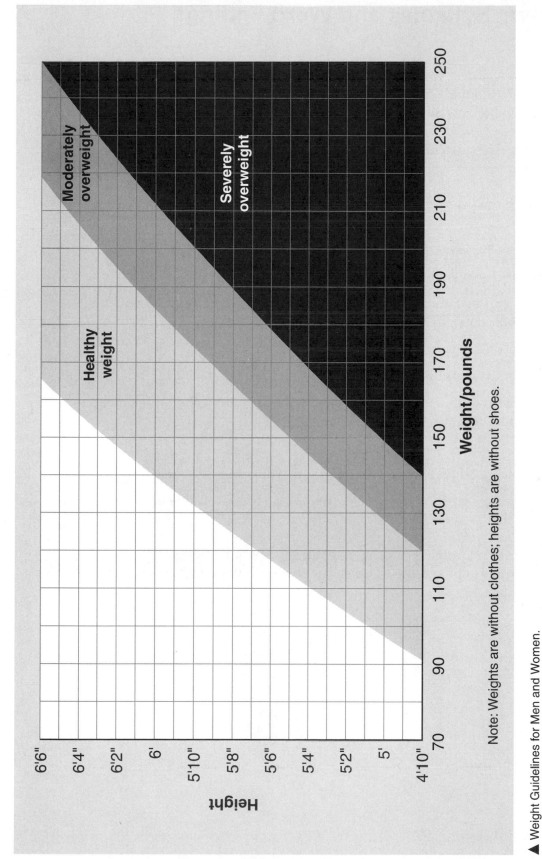

Height

6'6"
6'4"
6'2"
6'
5'10"
5'8"
5'6"
5'4"
5'2"
5'
4'10"

Moderately overweight

Healthy weight

Severely overweight

70 90 110 130 150 170 190 210 230 250

Weight/pounds

Note: Weights are without clothes; heights are without shoes.

▲ Weight Guidelines for Men and Women.

Source: U.S. Department of Agriculture and U.S. Department of Health and Human Services, *Dietary Guidelines for Americans, Fourth Edition 1995.*

Oral Review: Syllables and Word Endings

Name: _____ Date: _____

Schedule an individual consultation with your teacher, submit the review on tape, or complete the review as a pair project in which you dictate your sentences to your partner.

Complete each statement orally. Do *not* write and read your sentence completions.

1. My adviser never arranges meetings between 9:00 A.M. and 5:00 P.M.; she usually . . .

2. After he exercises, he always takes a shower and . . .

3. AIDS was discovered in the early 1980s. Since then . . .

4. Twenty years ago, most people communicated by telephone and mail; now almost everyone . . .

5. When the offices were being painted, all of the employees . . .

6. She was so happy about her grades that she . . .

7. Most professors in the United States expect their students to participate in discussions; most professors in my country . . .

8. Because he does not have a car, he . . .

9. I was wrong. I didn't think the rent included any utilities, but it . . .

10. I have been confused many times in the United States, but I was most confused the time that . . .

Rewind your tape. Monitor your word endings, especially the *-s* and *-ed* endings, in both the beginnings and the completions of your sentences. Make corrections at the end of your tape.

Chapter  5

Stress in Words (Part 1)

In every word of two or more syllables, one of the syllables is stronger than the others. Notice the strongest or STRESSED syllable in each of the following words:

FI nal   pro FES sor   dem o CRAT ic   vo CAB u lar y

What makes a syllable sound emphasized or stressed in American English? A combination of these three features creates syllable stress:

- **Length:** The vowel in the stressed syllable is longer. Which vowel sound is the longest in *meth od?*
- **Pitch:** The stressed syllable has a higher pitch. Which syllable has the higher pitch in *ap peal?*
- **Clear Vowel:** The stressed syllable has a full, clear vowel. Which syllable has the full, clear vowel in *ca pa ble?*

  Vowels in unstressed syllables are weak or reduced. They often sound like the neutral vowel sound /ə/ as in *a*bout.

  Why is syllable stress important? Listeners rely on stress patterns to help them identify words. The more frequently you misuse stress, the more effort listeners have to make to understand what you are saying.

  The next two chapters will help you improve your ability to predict and use stress patterns in words.

Listen!

Listening Activity 1

Listen to the speaker on tape or your teacher say one of the words from each pair. Put a check next to the word you hear.

1. _____ greenhouse   _____ green house
2. _____ selfish   _____ sell fish
3. _____ differentiated   _____ different shaded
4. _____ decade   _____ decayed
5. _____ pronouns   _____ pronounce
6. _____ orders   _____ hors d'oeuvres
7. _____ attic   _____ a tick
8. _____ one person   _____ one percent

9. _____ lookout   _____ Look out!

10. _____ homesick (sick *for* home)   _____ home sick (sick *at* home)

Check your answers with your teacher.

Now listen to *both* items in each pair. Can you hear the difference between them?

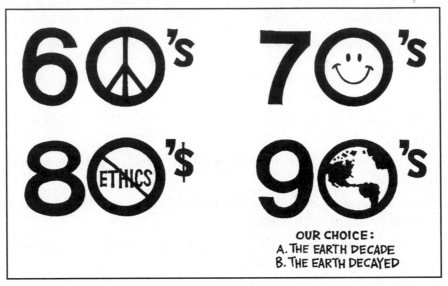

Wicks/*The Newhall Signal/*Rothco. Reprinted by permission.

Listening Activity 2

Ask an American English speaker to say each word below or listen carefully to the speaker on the tape. Underline the *stressed* syllable—the syllable that is longer, clearer, and higher in pitch. (Remember that if you ask a native speaker to say the words in sentences, the pronunciation will probably sound more natural.)

Example: pessimistic

1. volunteer
2. himself
3. survey (noun)
4. increase (noun)
5. recall (verb)
6. software
7. air conditioner

8. economy
9. economical
10. electricity
11. electrical
12. estimate
13. estimating
14. estimated

Check your answers with your teacher.

Note: Some words with more than one syllable have more than one stress. In the word *university,* the third ("ver") syllable has the strongest, or primary, stress. The first ("u") syllable has a weaker, or secondary, stress. In clear speaking, the primary stress is the most important.

Listening Activity 3

In this activity, listen to *un*stressed syllables. They are softer, shorter in length, and lower in pitch. Unstressed syllables are often pronounced with the schwa vowel sound "uh" or /ə/: METH od = /mɛθ əd/.

Listen to your teacher or the speaker on tape say the following words. Each time you hear the neutral schwa /ə/, put a line through the vowel.

Examples: METH ød   cøm PUTE   bi ø LOG í cál

1. con SULT ant
2. IN dus try
3. pro FES sion al
4. com MU ni ty
5. col LECT ed

6. PRE si dent
7. de LI cious
8. po LIT i cal
9. DEM on strate
10. a POL o gize

Check your answers in your dictionary. How many different vowels sounded like schwa?

Rules and Practices:
Using Parts of Speech to Predict Stress

Many words in English have no systematic rules for stressed and unstressed syllables. Other words have rules that are too complicated to be useful.

You can sometimes determine where stress falls in a word on the basis of its part of speech. In other words, recognizing that a word is a noun or a verb can sometimes help you with syllable stress.

The following guidelines will help you predict stress in words. Remember that these are guidelines and that no rule is foolproof!

Rule 5-1

Listen to the stress in compound nouns. Can you identify a pattern?

deadline	establish a deadline
classroom	a noisy classroom
software	install the software

☑ *Stress the first word in the compound more than the second word.*

Examples: AIRport, LAPtop

Note: Some speakers use /ə/ and others use /ɪ/ in unstressed syllables. Not all unstressed vowels sound like /ə/ or /ɪ/, but many do. In fact, most vowels in unstressed syllables adjacent to stressed syllables sound like /ə/ or /ɪ/ to make a clear distinction between stressed and unstressed syllables.

Rule 5-2

Listen to these two-noun compounds. Where is the stress?

air conditioner	repair the air conditioner
traffic jam	stuck in a traffic jam
air pollution	causes of air pollution

✔ ***Stress often falls on the first noun (or the main syllable of the first noun).***
Examples: VAcuum cleaner, comPUter lab

Rule 5-3

Listen to these reflexive pronouns. Where is the stress?

myself	went by myself
themselves	finished it themselves

✔ ***Stress -self or -selves.***
Example: herSELF

Rule 5-4

Listen to ten and teen numbers like *forty* and *fourteen*. Do you hear a regular pattern of stress?

sixty candles / sixteen candles

gate 40 / gate 14

May thirtieth / May thirteenth

✔ ***Stress the -teen syllable.***
Example: EIGHty versus eighTEEN

A HELPFUL HINT

Sometimes native speakers of American English do not give strong stress to the ***-teen*** syllable. As a result, you may have trouble distinguishing "He is eighteen years old" from "He is eighty years old."

Here is another clue to help you hear the difference. The /t/ at the beginning of stressed syllables, like ***-teen,*** has a sharp, clear /t/ sound. The /t/ at the beginning of unstressed syllables in the middle of words, like ***-ty,*** sounds more like /d/—EIGHdy, THIRdy, SIXdy.

Exercise 1

Say the following noun compounds with the speaker on tape or take turns saying them with a partner. The most important signal of stress is length, so s-t-r-e-t-c-h, or prolong, your stressed syllables.

Suggestion: Add movement to your pronunciation practice. Start with a closed fist. As you say the words below, open your fist on the stressed syllables and close it on the unstressed syllables.

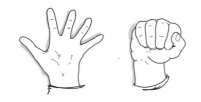

Examples: V-O-I-C-E   mail

         R-E-S-T   room

        W-O-R-D   processor

SIMPLE COMPOUNDS

sunglasses	earthquake	teenager
newspaper	football	classroom
workbook	headache	roommate
backpack	popcorn	mailbox
toothbrush	haircut	software

TWO-NOUN COMPOUNDS

seat belt	television station	office party
stock market	Web page	space shuttle
toilet paper	file cabinet	jet lag
coffee table	air bag	heart attack
health care	service charge	computer search

Choose three compounds you use frequently and write typical sentences you might say with them. Dictate your sentences to your partner.

1. _____

2. _____

3. _____

Exercise 2

Do you know these facts? With a partner, guess the correct statistic in each sentence.

Listen to your teacher or the speaker on tape read the sentences with the correct answers. Circle the answers. Take turns practicing the sentences.

1. (17/70) percent of all smokers want to quit.

2. A typical bath uses (15/50) gallons of water.

3. About (13/30) percent of all births in the United States are to single mothers.

4. In 1995, about (14/40) percent of Florida's population was foreign born.

5. About (15/50) percent of all fatal car crashes are alcohol related.

6. Around (15/50) percent of Americans say they are shy.

7. Approximately (17/70) percent of Americans donate to charities.

8. Friday the (13th, 30th) is considered an unlucky date.

9. In 1995, (14/40) percent of all U.S. households owned personal computers.

Exercise 3

Close your book and listen to your teacher or the speaker on tape ask the question. Give the answer. Then listen to your teacher or the speaker on tape give the answer. Were your stress patterns correct?

Or you can work with a partner. One student asks the question; the other student closes the book and gives the answer.

Examples:

What do you call . . . ?

a pot for coffee	(COFfee pot)
games on video	(VIDeo games)

1. a store that sells groceries   (GROcery store)

2. paper for notes   (NOTEpaper)

3. paper with news   (NEWSpaper)

4. a driver of a cab   (CAB driver)

5. a driver of a bus   (BUS driver)

(Switch roles.)

6. a knife for steak   (STEAK knife)

7. a spoon for tea   (TEAspoon)

8. a club you visit at night   (NIGHTclub)

9. an appliance for washing dishes   (DISHwasher)

10. a storm with thunder   (THUNderstorm)

Rule 5-5

Listen to each verb with a prefix and a base. Can you identify the stress pattern?

outrun	outrun his teammate
overlook	overlook the error
withdrew	withdrew fifty dollars
predict	predict the outcome

☑ *Stress the base, or the second element, of these verbs.*

Examples: underSTAND, overEAT, interACT

Rule 5-6

Listen to the stress patterns in these two-word phrasal verbs. Which word has stronger stress?

print out	print out the document
put off	put off the meeting
brush up	brush up on my Spanish

☑ *Stress the particle, or second element, more strongly.*

Examples: get OUT, look UP

Practice the stress pattern in these two-word phrasal verbs. Review *-ed* endings and linking.

passed OUT	counted DOWN
pointed OUT	figured OUT
dropped OFF	worked OUT

Note: Sometimes phrasal verbs have noun equivalents. Compare the noun and verb forms.

NOUN	VERB
Here's the *PRINTout.*	I *printed* it *OUT.*
She's a *DROPout.*	She *dropped OUT.*
Let's get *TAKEout.*	Let's *take* it *OUT.*

Rule 5-7

Listen to these compound adverbs indicating location or direction. Where is the stress?

overseas	go overseas
downtown	drove downtown
northeast	in the northeast

✔ ***Stress the second part of the compound adverb.***

Examples: outSIDE, upSTAIRS

Rule 5-8

Listen to these two-syllable words used as both nouns and verbs. Do you hear a pattern in the placement of stress?

NOUN	VERB
conduct	conduct
present	present
record	record
rebel	rebel

✔ ***Stress the first syllable in nouns and the second syllable in verbs.***

Examples: CONvert (noun), conVERT (verb)

Listen to the noun-verb pairs once more. What happened to the vowel sound in the first syllable of each verb?

SOMETHING TO THINK ABOUT

Think about what you have learned in this chapter.
Can you create a general rule for stress in nouns?
Can you create a general rule for stress in verbs?

Exercise 4

Say the following noun-verb pairs with the speaker on tape or work with a partner as follows. Student 1 says one word from each noun-verb pair. If student 1 says a verb, student 2 says the same word as a noun and vice versa.

Example: Student 1 says . . . proDUCE.
Student 2 says . . . PROduce.

NOUN	VERB	NOUN	VERB
convict	convict	checkout	check out
conduct	conduct	handout	hand out
insult	insult	strikeout	strike out
produce	produce	ripoff	rip off
object	object	takeover	take over
project	project	makeup	make up
suspect	suspect	workout	work out
recall	recall	cutback	cut back

Exercise 5

Say the words and sentences below. After you say each sentence, listen to your teacher or the speaker on tape say the same sentence. Were your stress patterns correct?

1. (pay back)   I'll pay you back next week.

2. (paycheck)   I deposited my paycheck.

3. (newspaper)   Recycling newspaper is a good idea.

4. (checkbook)   My checkbook has disappeared.

5. (dropout)   She's a high school dropout.

6. (outgrown)   He's already outgrown his new shoes.

7. (upstairs)   Room 210 is upstairs.

8. (give up)   Don't give up before you try.

9. (present)   I'll present the speaker.

10. (permit)   You'll need a permit to do the work.

11. (boyfriend/suspect)   Her boyfriend is a suspect.

12. (take off/thirty)   The plane's due to take off at 7:30.

13. (pick up)   I'll pick you up at seven.

14. (project)   Did they project our profits?

15. (homework/handout)   Your homework is on the handout.

Note: Some noun-verb pairs do not have stress shift (PROgram, misTAKE, PROfit, deBATE, rePORT, conCERN, and ANswer).

A HELPFUL HINT

When we use abbreviations and symbols for elements and compounds, all letters and numbers have full stress. The pitch glides down on the last letter or number.

Examples: C̅ D̅ (Compact Disc)
M̅ A̅ (Master of Arts)
E̅ T̅ (Extraterrestrial)

If a speaker says three or more stressed syllables in sequence, the rate of speech slows significantly.

Examples: M̅ B̅ A̅ (Master of Business Administration)
T̅ G̅ I̅ F̅ (Thank Goodness It's Friday)
Y̅ M̅ C̅ A̅ (Young Men's Christian Association)

Exercise 6

Write the abbreviations and symbols for the following.

Say each abbreviation and then listen to the speaker on tape say it. Or take turns saying the abbreviations with a partner. Monitor your partner.

1. _____ Los Angeles
2. _____ intelligence quotient
3. _____ water
4. _____ carbon dioxide
5. _____ parental guidance
6. _____ automatic teller machine
7. _____ certified public accountant
8. _____ cardiopulmonary resuscitation
9. _____ very important person
10. _____ chief executive officer
11. _____ grade point average
12. _____ bacon, lettuce, and tomato (sandwich)
13. _____ International Monetary Fund
14. _____ John Fitzgerald Kennedy
15. _____ public relations

What do these abbreviations mean?

16.

NEW YEAR
CELEBRATION
Dec. 31
9:00

The NELSONS

R.S.V.P. REGRETS
270-3256

17.

FYI
Here is a
draft of the
report.
Jim

18.

Peggy,
Call home
ASAP.
Bev

Communicative Practice: Solving a Problem

InfoGap

Your bank, National Bank of Illinois (NBI), has notified you that your account has insufficient funds to cover the most recent check you wrote. Your records are incomplete but indicate that you have enough money in your account. Call the bank to find the error.

You, the customer, have your checkbook (shown in the figure on page 139). Your partner, a bank officer, has a printout of the canceled checks (listed in the figure on page 140). Compare your records item by item and fill in any missing information. Remember that this is a phone conversation and you cannot see each other's records.

Preview stress patterns in key terms. Lengthen the stressed syllables:

AT&T	drugstore	traffic court	sixteen
NBI	MasterCard	airline ticket	fifteen
ATM	CheckCard	check number	fifty
USA	bookstore	account number	thirty
TWA	payroll	service charge	thirteen
	haircut		forty
	Supercuts		
	Riverdale		

PRIME-TIME PRACTICE

Oral Journal

What regular household chores do you have to do? What errands do you have to run? What items do you have to pick up? Which tasks do you especially like or dislike and why?

Step 1: Preview stress patterns in key vocabulary below. Record yourself discussing these questions.

Sample key vocabulary: *housework, weekends, weekdays, clean up, put away, hang up, drop off, call up, throw away, take out, catch up, pick up, ATM, phone call, grocery store, drugstore, dish detergent, toothpaste, bedroom, bathroom*

Step 2: Listen to your tape. Note stress patterns in nouns and verbs. Write those you want to improve.

NOUNS	VERBS
_____	_____
_____	_____
_____	_____

Step 3: Record your response again. Listen and submit the tape to your teacher for feedback.

"Oral Review: Stress in Words" appears at the end of Chapter 6.

Chapter 6

Stress in Words (Part 2)

In Chapter 5, you used parts of speech to predict stress in words. Another way to predict stress is with suffixes or word endings. Many suffixes, like *-ity, -ic,* and *-ee*, create predictable patterns of word stress.

Listen to your teacher say the sets of words below. Can you hear a regular pattern of stress in each set?

1. facility	credibility	minority	objectivity
2. athletic	traumatic	historic	atomic
3. guarantee	referee	absentee	degree

Now say the words with your teacher.

1. faCILity	crediBILity	miNORity	objecTIVity
2. athLETic	trauMATic	hisTORic	aTOMic
3. guaranTEE	refeREE	absenTEE	deGREE

In this chapter, you will learn some general guidelines for suffixes and word stress. These guidelines will help you pronounce new words more accurately, especially long academic, scientific, and technical terms that come from Latin and Greek.

Listen!

Listening Activity

Listen to your teacher or the speaker on tape read the passage two times. The first time, close your book and listen for meaning. The second time, write the missing words in the spaces below.

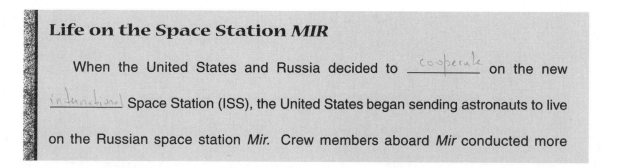

Life on the Space Station *MIR*

When the United States and Russia decided to ___cooperate___ on the new

___international___ Space Station (ISS), the United States began sending astronauts to live

on the Russian space station *Mir*. Crew members aboard *Mir* conducted more than 200 _scientific_ experiments. These experiments provided valuable data for

the _operation_ of the ISS. The most valuable lessons, however, were learned

through hardships and mishaps aboard the Russian space station.

Unlike the luxurious spaceships depicted in movies, *Mir* was small, crowded, and

chaotic. The central compartment was a tube filled with _____ and

cramped _____ living in zero _____. Crew members wore the same

clothes for two weeks. They had to recycle sweat for drinking water. Power

problems forced them to spend time in the dark. Problems with the cooling system

caused the _____ to rise and temperatures to reach 95 degrees Fahrenheit.

_____ problems between the ground and *Mir* resulted in the _____ to get

regular e-mail messages. The most _____ mishaps were a 14-minute fire and

a collision with the cargo freighter *Progress.*

All in all, *Mir* was a useful training ground for the ISS. NASA officials now realize

that ISS crew members need not only _____ training for _____ and

_____ research, but also wide-ranging _____ skills so that they can

_____ difficult living conditions and cope with unexpected problems.

Information adapted from Phillip Chien, "Space Jalopy," *Popular Science,* May 1998, p. 96;
Fred Guterl, "One Thing After Another," *Discover,* January 1998, p. 74; Daniel Goldin, Prepared
Testimony Before House Science Committee, February 5, 1998.

Check your answers with your teacher.

Mir

Rules and Practices:
Using Suffixes to Predict Stress

Rule 6-1

The same stress pattern applies to all the suffixes below. Listen to your teacher or the speaker on tape say the words. Try to identify the pattern.

a. -ic

scientific

organic

chaotic

b. -ify

solidify

personify

humidify

c. -graphy

photography

geography

biography

d. -ical

technological

economical

theoretical

e. -ogy

anthropology

psychology

biology

f. -ious, -eous

mysterious

suspicious

courageous

g. -ial

financial

official

commercial

h. -ity

minority

fatality

possibility

i. -tion, -sion

distribution

addiction

permission

j. -ian

technician

physician

Canadian

✔ *Stress the syllable immediately before the suffixes above.*

Examples: optiMIStic, huMANity, paTHOlogy, vegeTARian, inDUStrial

Rule 6-2

Listen to the words with suffixes like *-ee, -eer, -ese, -esque, -ique,* and *-ette.* What is the stress pattern?

volunteer	a volunteer effort
referee	referee the game
diskette	high-density diskette
Japanese	Japanese students

✔ *Stress the syllable with each of the suffixes above.*

Examples: engiNEER, pictuRESQUE, techNIQUE

Exercise 1

Part A: Fill in the blanks in the chart by adding suffixes *-ese, -ic, -ify, -ity, -tion, -ian,* or *-ogy.* Underline the syllables (or vowels) with the primary stresses. Compare your answers with those of your classmates.

Say the words with the speaker on tape or take turns saying the words with a partner. Nod your head slightly as you say the stressed syllables.

	Noun	Verb	Adjective
Examples: real	reality	realize	realistic
economy	economy economics	economize	economic economical
1. electric		electrify	electronic electrical
2. major		X	major
3. method	methodology	X	
4. person	personality		personal
5. photograph		photograph	photographic
6. Japan		X	
7. period	periodical periodicity	X	
8. philosophy	philosopher	philosophize	
9. mechanism		mechanize	mechanical
10. specify	specification	specify	

Note: Exceptions to Rules 6-1 and 6-2: (1) *-ic*—POlitics, RHEtoric, CAtholic; (2) *-sion*—TElevision; (3) *-ee*—comMITtee, COFfee.

Part B: Because stressed syllables have clear vowels, this is a good time to review the Vowel Chart in Appendix C. Each vowel sound on the chart has a number. Use the number to identify the vowel sound in each stressed syllable in Exercise 1.

         ①   ⑤   ①   ②

Examples: <u>real</u>   re<u>a</u>lity   <u>real</u>ize   real<u>is</u>tic

---

PRIME-TIME PRACTICE

In Chapter 2, you listed key words you want to pronounce clearly. Write those words and any others you have added to your list below. For each word, identify the vowel number in the syllable with the primary stress. Practice saying each word on your list with a full, clear vowel in the stressed syllable.

_____

_____

_____

_____

Rule 6-3

Approximately 1,000 English verbs end in the *-ate* suffix. These verbs are common in scientific, academic, and business contexts, and they have predictable stress patterns. Listen to your teacher or the speaker on tape say these verbs. Can you identify a pattern?

    exaggerate   associate   procrastinate

    innovate   integrate   subordinate

☑ *Stress the second syllable before the suffix.*

Examples: CALculate, MOtivate, conGRAtulate

Many learners of American English stress the *-ate* syllable. However, the second syllable before the suffix should be stressed (EStimate), even if an *-ed* (EStimated) or *-ing* (EStimating) is added. The stress shifts to another syllable only when *-ion* is added (estiMAtion). With practice, the pattern will become natural and automatic.

Repeat these examples:

    EStimate   EStimated   EStimating   EStimator   (estiMAtion)

    INdicate   INdicated   INdicating   INdicator   (indiCAtion)

    coORdinate   coORdinated   coORdinating   coORdinator   (coordiNAtion)

A HELPFUL HINT

Sometimes *-ate* words are adjectives, nouns, and adverbs, as well as verbs.

Adjective with *-ate:*	That's an **accurate** description.
Noun with *-ate:*	She's a **graduate** of M.I.T.
Adverb with *-ate:*	Send the order **immediately**.

In adjectives, nouns, and adverbs with *-ate,* the stress pattern is the same, but *-ate* sounds like the word *it.*

NOUN *(-ate = it)*	**VERB *(-ate = ate)***
Here is a **DUplicate** of the letter.	I need to **DUplicate** the letter.
He's going to give us an **EStimate**.	He's going to **EStimate** the cost.

Exercise 2

Practice saying the words in the chart. Check your pronunciation with the speaker on tape or have your partner monitor you. L-e-n-g-t-h-e-n the stressed syllables and just be relaxed about the unstressed syllables.

Then say the words in unison with your class. Snap your fingers on the stressed syllables.

Verb	Add *-ed*	Add *-ing*	Noun/Adj	Add *-ion*
1. graduate	GRAduated	GRAduating	GRAduate	graduAtion
2. associate	associated	associating	associate	association
3. demonstrate	demonstrated	demonstrating	X	demonstration
4. differentiate	differentiated	differentiating	X	differentiation
5. separate	separated	separating	separate	separation

Exercise 3

With a partner, apply what you know about stress patterns in words and say the word sequences below. Use the words to create sentences. Take turns saying the sentences. Monitor your partner's stress patterns. Remember *-s* and *-ed* endings.

Example: problem – illustrate – handout
            The problem is illustrated in your handout.

   1. roommate – graduate – June fifteenth

   2. post office – locate – Peachtree Street

3. candidate – position – energetic – ambitious

4. mechanic – estimate – cost – repair

5. decorate – cake – birthday

6. risky – speculate – stock market

7. simple – operate – new software

8. governments – send – delegates – UN

9. supervisor – delegate – authority – employees

10. countries – negotiate – agreement

Communicative Practice: Library Orientation

You have the key (page 141) to the location of various areas of the library on the three floors. Your partner has a map of the library (page 142) with only a letter designating each area.

Your partner should look at the list below the map and report to you eight to ten areas of greatest interest. Circle those areas of interest on the Key to Location.

Then tell your partner the location of each area of interest by floor and letter. Your partner should write each area of interest in the appropriate blank on the map.

PRIME-TIME PRACTICE

Pronouncing Unfamiliar Words
Use what you know about stress to pronounce long, difficult words you may be seeing for the first time.

Step 1: In the following announcement, use rules from Chapters 5 and 6 to predict the pronunciation of the boldfaced words. If you are not sure of a pronunciation, check your dictionary.

Step 2: Imagine that you are talking with a classmate or colleague on the phone. Use the announcement to share information about the conference. Record your explanation on tape. (Do not simply read the announcement.)

Step 3: Listen to your tape. Monitor your pronunciation of the boldfaced words. Make corrections at the end of the tape.

Announcing . . .

MEDICAL INFORMATICS: COMPUTER **APPLICATIONS** IN **HEALTH CARE**
Conference Center/University Hospital
April **14th**

1:30   **Keynote**
        "Improving **Quality** of Care Through Improved **Medical Records**
        Technology"
2:30   **Workshops** (open to all **attendees**)
        1. "**Electronic** Patient **Records**"
        2. "**Security** and **Confidentiality** of **Information**"
        3. "**Integrated Clinical** and **Financial** Systems"
        4. "**Software Engineering**"
5:30   **Reception – Ballroom**

See our **Web site** for **registration information:** www.shortcourse.**edu**

Extend Your Skills . . . to Small-Group Discussions

You are a member of the International Olympic Committee (IOC). It is your job to select a suitable city for the next Summer Olympic Games.

Arrange yourselves in groups of four or five. Each person in your group should select his or her favorite city in the world to be the choice for hosting the next Summer Olympic Games. Write your choice and the choices of the other group members in the chart on the next page. As you work through the categories on the chart, evaluate the city of your choice on a scale of 1 to 5:

5-excellent   4-good   3-average   2-fair   1-poor

Discuss and defend your ratings as you work through the categories. Add up total points (maximum score is 50) and try to reach consensus on the best candidate.

Preview the stress patterns in key terms: Practice these words from the chart on the next page. Remember that your stressed syllables need l-e-n-g-t-h.

airport	nightclubs	accessibility	accommodations
airlines	table tennis	quality	transportation
baseball	water polo	stability	
volleyball	street crime	humidity	
freeways		hospitality	
subways			
forecast			
weightlifting			

	5 = excellent 4 = good 3 = average 2 = fair 1 = poor		(name of city)	(name of city)	(name of city)	(name of city)	(name of city)

CATEGORIES AND COMMENTS	YOUR CITY	1	2	3	4
Accessibility — Airport/airlines:					
Accommodations — Number/quality of hotel rooms:					
Transportation — Freeways/subways/ taxicabs:					
Entertainment — Restaurants/ nightclubs:					
Sports Facilities — For swimming, track, baseball, basketball, volleyball, table tennis, water polo, field hockey, sailing, weightlifting, etc.:					
Languages — Number spoken:					
Political Stability of Country:					
Security — Street crime/police force:					
Weather — July forecast/humidity:					
Other — Corporate support/ hospitality/medical facilities/ other unique aspects of the city:					
TOTAL SCORES					

Adapted from chart by staff accompanying "Grading the Competition: Atlanta," *Atlanta Journal and Constitution,* July 15, 1990, p. A-1. Reprinted with permission from the *Atlanta Journal* and the *Atlanta Constitution.*

Summarize your group's bid on the following Outline for Bid. Select a spokesperson to present the bid to the class in two minutes or less.

As you present the strengths, introduce new categories with transition words and phrases, such as *one positive point, next,* and *in addition.* See the outline for a list of useful transitions.

Be sure to provide specific examples to make your bid interesting. For example, if your city received a rating of **excellent** in the category *Languages,* mention the languages spoken in that city.

In your summary, indicate that you have fully considered your choice by mentioning one weak area. Finish your summary, however, with another mention of the one or two greatest strengths; your listeners are likely to remember what they hear last. After the groups present their bids, the class can select the most convincing presentation.

OUTLINE FOR BID

Useful Phrases

We'd like to nominate . . .	Top candidate: Points:
Our candidate for . . .	
	Strengths:
First . . .	**1.**
Next . . .	**2.**
In addition . . .	
Another positive aspect . . .	**3.**
	4.
The greatest strength . . .	
Finally . . .	**5.**
In summary . . .	Summary:
In conclusion . . .	**1.** One weakness:
In closing . . .	**2.** Two greatest strengths:

Oral Review: Stress in Words

Name: _____ Date: _____

Schedule an individual consultation with your teacher or submit the review on tape.

Part A

- Predict the stressed syllables in the boldfaced words.
- Record the sentences.
- Listen to your tape and underline the syllables you stressed. Did you stress the correct syllables? Were your stressed syllables longer and clearer than your unstressed syllables?
- Make corrections at the end of the tape.

1. The **Southeast** is famous for its **hospitality.**
2. You'll get a **certificate** on **completion** of the course.
3. I'd like a **hamburger** and a **milkshake.**
4. He's **suspected** of **carjacking.**
5. We plan to **present** an award to her.
6. I can't **figure out** the problem by **myself.**
7. You're not **permitted** to park here without a **permit.**
8. We expect a **substantial increase** in salary.
9. John is one of the new **corporate** officers.
10. He's working on a **degree** in **pharmacology.**

Part B

Record yourself reading the passage "Life on the Space Station *Mir*" in the Listening Activity at the beginning of the chapter. Listen to the tape. Monitor for word stress and make corrections at the end.

BEYOND THE PRONUNCIATION CLASSROOM

Applying for a Library Card*

Now that you are becoming more comfortable with new pronunciation patterns, each chapter will end with a Beyond the Pronunciation Classroom. In this section, you will apply pronunciation points to everyday interactions with native speakers.

Pronunciation Point: Stress patterns in words.

Task: Go to the public library and apply for a library card.

- Take appropriate I.D. (driver's license, checkbook, or utility bill). Call first and ask what you will need.

- Find out the lending period for various items (books, CDs, and videotapes).

- Ask about the fine for overdue materials (15 cents/30 cents/50 cents a day?).

Before: With your class, anticipate the interaction. Preview the stress patterns in key words and rehearse with your partner the language you might need.

KEY VOCABULARY	STRESS PATTERN
I.D.	_____
checkbook	_____
utility bill	_____
driver's license	_____
CDs	_____
videotapes	_____
overdue	_____
fifteen cents	_____
fifty cents	_____

After: Discuss your experience with your class.

*This task was suggested by Josie Kramer, 1999 TESOL Summer Academy, Johns Hopkins University.

Midcourse Self-Evaluation

Part A: Circle the answers.   (1 = not at all . . . 5 = very much)

1. My general awareness of English
   speech patterns has improved.   1   2   3   4   5

2. I have a better idea of why I am
   sometimes not understood.   1   2   3   4   5

3. I am beginning to hear problems
   in my own speech.   1   2   3   4   5

4. My speech is beginning to improve.   1   2   3   4   5

5. I want to improve my intelligibility. 1   2   3   4   5

6. I have worked hard to improve my
   intelligibility.   1   2   3   4   5

Part B: In an AUDIO JOURNAL, answer these questions.

1. In what ways has my speech improved?

2. What are three areas in which I want my speech to improve before the end of
   the course?

   a. _____

   b. _____

   c. _____

3. What will I have to do to achieve these changes?

4. What is one speaking situation in which I want my speech to improve?

Chapter 7

Rhythm in Sentences

Every language has its own rhythm or beat. Two very different rhythm patterns are represented in the illustrations below.

If a child were dragging a stick along a picket fence made of slats of uniform size and spacing, the rhythm pattern would be regular. Clap the rhythm pattern you see.

▲ In some languages, every syllable has more or less equal emphasis.

If another child were dragging a stick along a picket fence made of slats of varying sizes and spacings, the rhythm pattern would be less uniform. Clap the rhythm pattern you see.

▲ In other languages, some syllables are strong and others are weak.

Which figure represents the rhythm of your language? Which figure represents the rhythm of English?

In the previous two chapters, you learned about stressed and unstressed syllables in words. The combination of stressed and unstressed syllables helps create the **rhythm** of English. In this chapter, you will learn about the rhythm patterns in phrases, sentences, and longer stretches of speech.

SOMETHING TO THINK ABOUT

Speakers of American English sometimes give full stress to every word when they are angry or adamant.

Example: THIS PAPER WAS DUE ON MONDAY.

If you have a tendency to stress every word and syllable equally, you might sound abrupt, angry, or impatient without intending to.

Listen!

Listening Activity 1

Just as words have stressed and unstressed syllables, so do phrases and sentences.

Listen to your teacher or the speaker on tape say these word/phrase pairs. In each pair, the rhythm pattern of the word is repeated in the phrase.

Example: re JEC ted   He WRECKED it.

WORDS	PHRASES
1. engineer	He was here.
2. overthrow	In a row.
3. himself	An elf.
4. convert (verb)	He's hurt.
5. presented	She sent it.
6. progressed	The best.
7. permit (noun)	Learn it.
8. volunteer	She can hear.

If you did not hear the rhythm, rewind the tape and listen again with your eyes closed.

Listening Activity 2

Each box on the next page has three phrases. Each phrase has a *different* number of syllables but takes the *same* length of time to say. Listen to your teacher or the speaker on tape say the phrases.

TIME

BROAD	VIEW
BROAD	reVIEW
BROADer	reVIEW

SLOW	TURN
SLOWly	TURN
SLOWly	reTURN

NEW	VICE
NEW	deVICE
NEWest	deVICE

QUICK	CALL
QUICK	reCALL
QUICKly	reCALL

Did you notice that some syllables were long and others were short and hurried?

Say the phrases with your teacher or the speaker on tape. Tap the two strong beats in each phrase with the speaker. Make the stressed syllables fall *on* the beats and the unstressed syllables fit *between* the beats.

Listening Activity 3

Poems and rhymes are one way to acquire rhythm patterns. Listen to your teacher or the speaker on tape say these lines from popular English rhymes for children. Pay attention to the rhythm, not the words. Write the number of strong beats in each line.

Three blind mice!	3
See how they run!	_____
They all ran after the farmer's wife,	_____
She cut off their tails with a carving knife.	_____
Did you ever see such a sight in your life	_____
As three blind mice?	_____

One, two,	_____
Buckle my shoe;	_____
Three, four,	_____
Knock at the door;	_____
Five, six,	_____
Pick up sticks;	_____
Seven, eight,	_____
Lay them straight.	_____

Listening Activity 4

 Listen to the incomplete dialogue below. Even though more than half of the words are missing, can you understand the dialogue?

CUSTOMER: __Is__ __it__ possible __to__ fly __to__ Los Angeles __on__ Sunday?

AGENT: Yes, __there__ __are__ __a__ couple __of__ flights. One __is__ __at__ 9:30 __in__ __the__ other __is__ __at__ 3:15.

CUSTOMER: What __is__ __the__ fare __in__ coach?

AGENT: __the__ round-trip fare _____ $318.00 plus tax. __do__ __you__ want __to__ make __a__ reservation?

 Now listen to the full dialogue. Fill in the blanks with the words you hear.

Check your answers with your teacher. What kinds of words did you write? Were these words strong or weak in the dialogue?

PRIME-TIME PRACTICE

Listen to native speakers of English on television. Pay attention to *how* they speak, rather than to *what* they say.

1. Listen to rhythm patterns in a news broadcast. Do you hear strong beats and weak beats?

2. Notice the weak, unstressed words. Are they hard to understand? Are they necessary for understanding?

3. Watch a few minutes of a TV drama or sitcom without the sound. Notice body movement. Turn the sound on. Notice the connection between movement and the stressed parts of the message. Do you see more eye, head, upper body, or arm movement?

Write your observations and discuss them with your classmates and your teacher.

Rules and Practices:
Stressed and Reduced Words

Listeners of English expect certain words to be strong and others to be weak. The strong words are the ones listeners pay attention to the most. Sharply contrasting stronger words with weaker, more obscure words is an important part of clear communication.

In the "Listen!" section, you listened to stressed words and unstressed words.

What kinds of words were stressed? _____

What kinds of words were unstressed? _____

Read the guidelines that follow. How do they compare with what you wrote?

Rule 7-1

✔ *Stress important content words like these:*

NOUNS	VERBS	ADJECTIVES	ADVERBS
LUNCH	VOTE	CHEAP	QUITE
ANswer	exPLAIN	ACTive	REALly

NEGATIVES	WH-QUESTION WORDS	DEMONSTRATIVES
CAN'T	WHAT	THIS
NOT	HOW	THOSE

Examples: The LUNCH was CHEAP.
He WON'T GIVE me an ANswer.

Note: In content words of more than one syllable like *ANswer*, stress the appropriate syllable.

Rule 7-2

✔ *Reduce or weaken function words. Function words serve a grammatical purpose, but they don't carry as much meaning. Function words include the following:*

ARTICLES	CONJUNCTIONS	PREPOSITIONS	PRONOUNS	AUXILIARY VERBS
a	and	to	her	can
the	or	of	you	have

Examples: **a.** Contraction: JOHN 's an OLD FRIEND.
(is)

    b. Obscured Vowels: /Kn/ /yə/ SEE?
                     (Can) (you)

    c. Omitted Consonant: LET /əm/ GO.
                     (him)

Exercise 1

In the following sentences, put a line (—) through each function word. Then put a line (—) through each unstressed syllable in the content words.

Say the sentences with the speaker on tape or practice with a partner as follows: Say the sentences. Your partner should listen and write the number of strong beats in each sentence.

Example: I~~ can't under~~stand.   _____2_____

1. I can understand.   _____

2. Please pass the pepper.   _____

3. He wants to leave.   _____

4. Do it as quickly as possible.   _____

5. Thank you for calling.   _____

(Switch roles.)

6. I'm sorry I'm late.   _____

7. I'd like you to meet my sister.   _____

8. I'll see you on Monday.   _____

9. Do you know my number?   _____

10. Can you call me later?   _____

Exercise 2

Say the rhymes and sentences below with your teacher or with the speaker on tape. The rhythm of each rhyme is repeated in the sentences that follow it.

Rhyme A: THREE BLIND MICE
        (Please sit down.)
        (Come back soon.)
        (Hans can't go.)
        (Don't drive fast.)

        SEE HOW they RUN.
        (Don't use my name.)
        (John lost the disk.)
        (Tell Mai I called.)
        (That book is good.)

Rhyme B: HICKory DICKory DOCK
               (Do it according to plan.)
               (Give me a burger with cheese.)
               (Who is the man I should see?)

               The MOUSE ran UP the CLOCK.
               (I'd like to cash a check.)
               (She'd rather take the bus.)
               (I'll have her call you back.)

Rhyme C: TWINkle, TWINkle LITtle STAR,
               (Let me help you find your keys.)
               (Don't forget the bread and milk.)
               (Tell me why you don't agree.)

               HOW I WONder WHAT you ARE.
               (Find a space and park your car.)
               (Thanks a lot for all your help.)
               (Don't forget to leave a tip.)

Did you notice that you had to compress and weaken unstressed words and syllables to maintain the rhythm patterns?

Exercise 3

With your teacher or the speakers on tape, step on the strong beats—just as Dorothy, the Scarecrow, and the Tinman did in the *The Wizard of Oz.*

	1	2	3	4
	LIons and	TIgers and	BEARS	oh MY
	LIons and	TIgers and	BEARS	oh MY

These words are longer, but the time between the strong beats is the same.

	1	2	3	4
	ELephants and	CROcodiles and	PYthons	oh MY
	ELephants and	CROcodiles and	PYthons	oh MY

Now try these lists. Keep the same strong beat regardless of the number of syllables.

	1	2	3	4
Miseries:	comPUters and	HOMEwork and	SCHEdules	oh MY (2×)
Pleasures:	SPRINGtime and	HOlidays and	CHOcolate	oh MY (2×)
Courses:	biOlogy and	ecoNOmics and	CHEmistry	oh MY (2×)
Occupations:	engiNEERS and	meCHAnics and	DENtists	oh MY (2×)

Fill in each blank with one word. Practice with your partner.

	1	2	3	4
Miseries:	_____ and	_____ and	_____ oh MY	
Pleasures:	_____ and	_____ and	_____ oh MY	
Others:	_____ and	_____ and	_____ oh MY	

A HELPFUL HINT

Try to overcome any resistance you have to sounding like a native speaker of English. Such resistance can limit pronunciation progress. Changing pronunciation, especially stress and rhythm, may involve changes in breathing, facial expression, and body movement. As a result, you might feel less Korean, Greek, Japanese, Chinese, Polish, Russian, French, Thai, Arabic, or Spanish, but be assured that you probably won't lose your accent completely. You will probably always sound like a native speaker of your language.

These suggestions may help:

1. Think of American English speakers you admire. Try to imitate their gestures and facial expressions, as well as their pronunciation patterns.

2. Imagine that your use of American English is like a change of clothes you can put on or take off, depending on the situation.

3. Remember that it is sufficient to change only those patterns that interfere with understanding and are highly distracting to the listener.

Exercise 4

Say the following phrases with your teacher or the speaker on tape.

In each set, phrase **a** is like a telegram and contains important content words. Phrases **b, c,** and so on have function words added but take the same length of time to say. Tap your pencil in time with the rhythm.

SAME TIME FOR EACH PHRASE

$\longleftarrow \qquad\qquad\qquad\qquad \longrightarrow$

	tap	*tap*
1. a.	FIre	KItchen.
b.	FIre in	KItchen.
c.	FIre in the	KItchen.
d.	a FIre in the	KItchen.
e.	There's a FIre in the	KItchen.

$\longleftarrow \qquad\qquad\qquad\qquad\qquad \longrightarrow$

	tap	*tap*	*tap*
2. a.	SNOW	exPECted	FRIday.
b.	SNOW is	exPECted	FRIday.
c.	SNOW is	exPECted on	FRIday.
d.	The SNOW is	exPECted on	FRIday.

$\longleftarrow \qquad\qquad\qquad\qquad\qquad \longrightarrow$

	tap	*tap*	*tap*
3. a.	reTURN	BOOKS	MONday.
b.	reTURN	BOOKS by	MONday.
c.	reTURN the	BOOKS by	MONday.
d.	I can reTURN the	BOOKS by	MONday.

Exercise 5

Make each sentence passive. With the speaker on tape or with your partner, say both the active and passive forms with the *same rhythm pattern.*

SAME TIME FOR EACH SENTENCE

$\longleftarrow \qquad\qquad\qquad\qquad\qquad\qquad \longrightarrow$

	tap	*tap*	*tap*
1.	SPIELberg	diRECted	E.T.
	E.T.	*was directed*	*by spielberg.*

2. GATES   FOUNDed   MIcrosoft.

_____

3. SOny   introDUCED   the WALKman.

_____

4. BELL   inVENTed   the TELephone.

_____

5. The BEAtles   SANG   "YESterday."

_____

PRIME-TIME PRACTICE

"Natural highs" are events or experiences that inspire us or make life enjoyable. Practice the simple rhythm patterns of the natural highs below. Read them into a tape recorder and add three of your own.

• Falling in love • Getting a letter • Going to the movies • Scoring the winning goal • Finishing a good book • Spending a day at the beach • Getting a surprise visit from a friend • Seeing a falling star • Getting a large tax refund • Having late night chats with an older brother or sister • Getting an A+ on a paper • Drinking a chocolate milkshake • Getting eight hours of sleep • Solving a problem • Getting a strike in bowling • Watching a beautiful sunset

• _____

• _____

• _____

Listen to your tape and monitor the rhythm patterns.

How do speakers of American English weaken or compress function words? On the next page are some common one-syllable function words and their unstressed pronunciations. These reductions are *not* errors. If you weaken these words, your speech will sound more natural. If you stress these words, your speech may sound monotonous.

Notice how many function words have schwa /ə/.

	Pronunciation	Examples
Articles		
a	/ə/	a mistake
the	/ðə/	on the desk
an	/ən/	an emergency
Conjunctions		
or	/ər/	pass or fail
and	/ən/ or /n/	hot and humid
Prepositions		
of	/ə/	deck of cards
	/əv/	out of eggs
to	/tə/	gone to lunch
for	/fər/	call for Pablo
at	/ət/	at home
Pronouns		
him	/əm/ or /ɪm/	tell him
her	/ər/	introduce her
them	/əm/	warn them
you	/yə/	are you tired?
Auxiliary Verbs		
do	/də/	what do you want?
can	/kən/ or /kn/	can you go?
have	/əv/ or /ə/	must have gone

Note: In some contexts, speakers may stress words that usually are weak.

He CAN'T SWIM, <u>CAN</u> he?   (in tag questions)

YES, he <u>IS</u> SICK.   (for special emphasis)

You will learn more about the influence of context in the next two chapters.

Exercise 6

Practice listening to unstressed function words. Fill in the blanks with the words you hear. (*Hint:* One of the missing words in each sentence is a reduced pronoun/auxiliary verb with a disappearing *h*: ̷him, ̷her, ̷his, ̷he, ̷has, or ̷have.)

Example: ____*Did*____ ____*he*____ get the promotion?

1. _____ _____ running in the marathon?

2. _____ _____ car be ready by this evening?

3. She's never used _____ credit cards.

4. He picked up _____ children.

5. I wish I could help _____ .

6. _____ _____ _____ gotten lost?

7. The interviewer asked _____ some questions.

8. He talked about _____ travels.

9. _____ _____ had two heart attacks.

10. That's what _____ said.

Exercise 7

Practice blending verb endings with reduced pronouns. Say the sentences after your teacher or the speaker on tape or take turns with a partner.

Example: confused him

| | (confuse-dəm) | **not** | confused/him |

1. blame-dəm   I blamed him for the accident.

2. check-dəm   I checked them out of the library.

3. drop-tər   I dropped her off at eight.

4. hand-zəm   She always hands them in on time.

5. keep-sər   Her new job keeps her busy.

6. look-təm   He looked him in the eye.

7. call-dər   Her roommate called her to the phone.

8. interview-dəm   I interviewed him for a job.

9. ask-tər   He asked her for change.

10. pay-zəm   The company pays them twice a month.

You will learn more about linking in Chapter 10.

A HELPFUL HINT

Students are frequently misunderstood when using the words *can* and *can't*. The word *can't* is stressed. It has a long, clear /æ/ vowel sound.

> *Example:* I CæN'T GO.

The word *can* is unstressed. It has an obscure /ə/ vowel or no vowel sound.

> *Examples:* I cən GO. (or)
> I cn GO.

To distinguish between *can't* and *can*, English speakers rely on stress/unstress, not on the presence/absence of *the /t/ sound*.

> *Examples:* I   can   TRUST him.
> I CAN'T TRUST him.

Exercise 8

Listen to the first verse of this chant. How many strong beats are in each line? ☐

CAN YOU DO ME A FAVOR?*

Verse 1: Can you do me a favor?
I can do you a favor.

Can you open the door?
I can open the door.

Can you turn out the light?
I can turn out the light.

Can you make it all right?
I can make it all right.

In the second verse, below, underline the strong beats. Then practice with your class. Half of the class asks the questions and the other half answers.

Verse 2: Can you take me to work?
I can take you to work.

Can you fly me to France?
I can fly you to France.

Can you press my pants?
I can press your pants.

Can you make it all right?
I can make it all right?

*Courtesy of Rebecca Samowitz, 1997 Summer Institute, American University.

With a partner, finish the third verse. Share it with the class.

Verse 3: Can you do me a favor?

I can do you a favor.

Can you _____?

_____.

_____?

_____.

_____?

_____.

Exercise 9

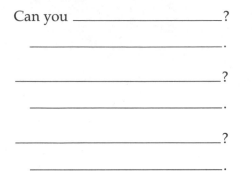

Listen to your teacher or the speaker on tape say the sentences below. Circle whether you hear the affirmative or the negative. Check your answers with your teacher.

Then with a partner, take turns reading the sentences in the affirmative or the negative. Your partner should respond in a way that shows understanding.

Example: Student 1 says . . . I (can, can't) go to the game.

Student 2 says . . . Why not?

1. I (can, can't) call you tomorrow.

2. I (can, can't) understand this equation.

3. She (can, can't) meet with me today.

4. He (can, can't) make an appointment tomorrow.

5. He (can, can't) come to the party.

6. You (were, weren't) told to do that.

7. The missing books (were, weren't) found.

8. We (were, weren't) here yesterday.

9. They (are, aren't) disappointed.

10. I (can, can't) be there by 9:00.

Communicative Practice: Scheduling an Appointment

InfoGap

Practice rhythm patterns as you work with a partner to schedule a mutually convenient business appointment.

Step 1: Preview the rhythm patterns in the sample sentences below. Pay special attention to *can* and *can't*.

> I can MEET on MONday at TEN.
>
> I can MEET from TWO to THREE.
>
> I CAN'T MEET you then. I'm GOing to the DENtist.
>
> Can you MEET at TWELVE?
>
> I'm BUsy from ONE to TWO.
>
> HOW about FRIday at TEN?

Step 2: Choose one of the following sets of roles. Decide who will play role A and who will play role B.

_____ **A.** Computer consultant

        B. Client

_____ **A.** Professor/Adviser

        B. Student research assistant

_____ **A.** Factory supervisor

        B. Vice president of production

_____ **A.** Accountant

        B. Client (Restaurant owner)

Step 3: Write the purpose of the appointment: _____

Step 4: In the calendars on pages 143 and 144, finish scheduling the shaded boxes with appointments typical for the role you are playing. Fill in schedule A for role A and schedule B for role B. Choose from the commitments below or create your own. **Leave unshaded boxes unscheduled**. Then sit back-to-back, initiate the phone call, tell your partner why you want to meet, and find a time when you are both free.

LIST OF COMMITMENTS		
director's meeting	workshop	aerobics class
out-of-town	lunch with CEO	staff meeting
conference	Japanese language class	lab work

Extend Your Skills . . . to Recording a Message

You have just purchased an answering machine for your home or office. Write a script for the outgoing message on your machine. Underline the content words (or the stressed syllables of the content words). Record your message. Listen to the tape and evaluate your rhythm patterns. Are your stressed words and syllables longer and stronger than your unstressed words and syllables?

Message:

_____

_____

_____

_____

_____

_____

_____ *(BEEP!)*

"Could you give me a moment to collect my thoughts? It's been some time since I spoke over the phone to an actual person."

Drawing by Joe Mirachi; © 1991 *The New Yorker Magazine*, Inc.
Reprinted by permission.

A HELPFUL HINT

Use what you have learned about rhythm when listening to spoken English. Pay attention to the parts of the message that carry the most information—the stressed parts. Don't worry about the unstressed, obscured parts. You do not have to hear unstressed words clearly to understand what is being said. Paying attention to the stressed information makes you a more efficient listener and leads you to the essence of the message.

Oral Review: Rhythm in Sentences

Schedule an individual consultation with your teacher, complete the review as a group project, or submit the review on tape.

DIRECTIONS: Mark the stressed words and syllables in these famous quotations. Read them with special attention to rhythm patterns.

WORDS OF WISDOM

1. A little learning is a dangerous thing.   —Alexander Pope

2. Imagination is the highest kite one can fly.   —Lauren Bacall

3. You are never fully dressed until you wear a smile.   —Charley Willey

4. A true friend is the best possession.   —Benjamin Franklin

5. Those who cannot remember the past are condemned to repeat it.
   —George Santayana

6. The secret of staying young is to live honestly, eat slowly, and lie about your age.   —Lucille Ball

7. It usually takes me more than three weeks to prepare a good impromptu speech.   —Mark Twain

8. I don't want to achieve immortality through my work. I want to achieve it through not dying.   —Woody Allen

9. Music is the universal language of mankind.
   —Henry Wadsworth Longfellow

10. The only thing we have to fear is fear itself.   —Franklin D. Roosevelt

Include your favorite "quotable quote" or words of wisdom. If you translate from your language, communicate the meaning in English as well as you can.

11. _____

Listen to your tape before you submit it. Did you emphasize the stressed words and syllables? Did you reduce the unstressed syllables and function words?

BEYOND THE PRONUNCIATION CLASSROOM

Knock! Knock! Jokes

"Knock! Knock!" jokes often play on reduced words and linking. These jokes are one way young children who are learning English as a first language become aware of these features of English rhythm.

Pronunciation Point: Rhythm, reduced words, and linking

Task: Ask a friend who is a native speaker whether she or he remembers a Knock! Knock! joke from childhood. Ask the friend to teach you one or two favorites. Write the jokes down.

Before: In small groups, analyze these jokes. What words are reduced? What words are linked? With a partner, practice telling the jokes.

X: Knock! Knock!	**X:** Knock! Knock	**X:** Knock! Knock!
Y: Who's there?	**Y:** Who's there?	**Y:** Who's there?
X: Letter.	**X:** Oliver.	**X:** The Sultan.
Y: Letter who?	**Y:** Oliver who?	**Y:** The Sultan who?
X: Letter in. It's cold out here!	**X:** Oliver friends are coming over.	**X:** The Sultan Pepper.

After: Bring jokes to class. Be prepared to teach a joke.

Chapter  8

Intonation and Focus in Discourse

In Chapter 7, you learned that function words are **unstressed** and that content words are **stressed.** One word or syllable in every phrase or sentence, however, receives more stress or emphasis than the others. This word is the most prominent word in the phrase and is called the *focus word*.

Notice how focus depends on context.

CONTEXT	FOCUS*
José looks relieved.	He FINished his rePORT.
Did José finish your report?	He FINished HIS rePORT.
José needs to write his report.	He FINished his rePORT.

When a conversation begins or a topic is introduced, the focus is usually the last content word or the stressed syllable of the last content word. Here are two utterances that might begin conversations:

Between passengers at the airport:

X: WHERE are you GOing?

Between a teenage child and a parent:

X: May I BORrow the CAR?

After a conversation has begun, the speaker can shift the focus to other words to highlight the new or important parts of the message.

Dialogue 1

X: WHERE are you GOing?

Y: To BOSton. WHERE are YOU going?

Dialogue 2

X: May I BORrow the CAR?

Y: WHICH car?

X: The NEW one.

*In this text, a large dot (•) signifies focus.

Focus is vital for clear communication because it signals information that is new or important in the discourse. In this chapter, you will learn guidelines for the placement of focus. You will also learn to highlight focus words by using *length* and *intonation*—the rise and fall of the pitch of the voice.

SOMETHING TO THINK ABOUT

Focus maintains the natural flow of communication between speakers and listeners. For example,

. . . if a colleague asked,

                  •
WHAT did you THINK of the MEETing?

. . . and you responded,

                  •
WHAT did you THINK of the MEETing?

. . . instead of shifting the focus from MEETing to YOU,

            •
WHAT did YOU think of the MEETing?

. . . your colleague might think that you had not heard the original question or that you were mimicking him or her.

Listen!

Listening Activity 1

Listen to this dialogue between college roommates. Put a dot (•) above the most prominent word in each phrase or thought group. Thought groups are separated with slash marks [/].

MIDTERM ANXIETY

              •   •
X: I've got to study. / Where've I put my book?

Y: Which book?

X: My calculus book.

Y: Try the bookcase.

X: The bookcase is full of your comic books.

Y: Then look in the bedroom.

X: I've looked in the bedroom. / I give up. / This apartment is a

     mess! / I can't find anything in this place.

Y: Wait a minute. / The book is right there / in your hand.

Check your answers with your teacher.

Listen to the speakers hum the dialogue. How did the speakers call attention to the most prominent element in each thought group?

Listening Activity 2

Listen to your teacher or the speaker on tape introduce a lecture on pollution. Put a dot (•) above the focus word (or the stressed syllable of the focus word) in each thought group.

> "Let's continue our discussion of pollution. / Yesterday we defined pollution. /
>
> Today we'll talk about the impact of pollution / . . . its far-reaching effects. / Many
>
> people think that pollution is just a problem for scientists / but it's not just a problem
>
> for scientists. / It's a problem that affects everyone. / Because it affects human lives /
>
> it's a health problem. / Because it affects property / it's an economic problem. / And
>
> because it affects our appreciation of nature / it's an aesthetic problem."

Check your answers with your teacher. What was the focus word in the first thought group? Why did it shift to a different word in the next thought group?

Listen again. What happens to the information *following* the focus in each thought group?

> "Let's conTINue our disCUSsion of polLUtion. / YESterday we deFINED
>
> polLUtion. / ToDAY we'll talk about the IMpact of polLUtion / . . . its FAR-REACHing
>
> efFECTS. / MAny PEOple THINK that polLUtion is just a PROBlem for SCIentists /
>
> but it's NOT just a PROBlem for scientists. / It's a PROBlem that afFECTS
>
> EVeryone. / Because it afFECTS HUman LIVES / it's a HEALTH PROBlem. /
>
> Because it afFECTS PROperty / it's an ecoNOmic PROBlem. / And because it
>
> afFECTS our appreciAtion of NAture / it's an aesTHEtic PROBlem."

Speakers of English organize speech into meaningful thought groups. Each thought group has one element that is most prominent; this element is longer and has a major pitch change.

Listening Activity 3

Listen to this dialogue. Notice the pitch change on the focus word. Do you hear (1) *falling intonation* ↘ or (2) *rising intonation* ↗ ?

DIALOGUE: ROOM SERVICE

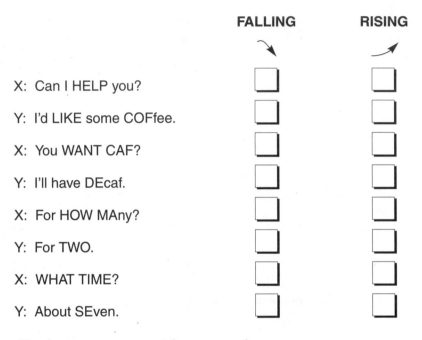

	FALLING ↘	RISING ↗
X: Can I HELP you?	☐	☐
Y: I'd LIKE some COFfee.	☐	☐
X: You WANT CAF?	☐	☐
Y: I'll have DEcaf.	☐	☐
X: For HOW MAny?	☐	☐
Y: For TWO.	☐	☐
X: WHAT TIME?	☐	☐
Y: About SEven.	☐	☐

Check your answers with your teacher.

Two basic intonation patterns are **falling** for making statements and asking *wh*-questions and **rising** for asking yes/no questions.

Note: Some books refer to *falling intonation* as *rising-falling intonation* because the pitch rises and then falls.

Example: Y: I'll have CAF. ↘

X: For how MAny? ↘

Y: For TWO. ↘

Rules and Practices: Placement of Focus

Rule 8-1

☑ *When a conversation begins or a topic is introduced, the most prominent word in the sentence—the word with the greatest pitch change—is usually the last content word. This is **neutral** focus.*

Examples: It's TIME to EAT.   Is it TIME to EAT?

WHEN did you GRAduate?   Did you GRAduate?

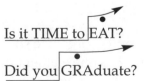

Note: If the prominent element is the last syllable, the pitch glides down.

HOW was your WEEK?

If the prominent element is not the last syllable, the pitch steps down.

HOW was your WEEKend?

Exercise 1

Practice neutral focus in sentences that might begin conversations. Repeat these sentences after your teacher or the speaker on tape.

A: Falling Intonation

Example: I LOST the KEYS.

1. HOW was your TRIP?

2. I NEED to apPLY for a CHECK Card.

3. I'd LIKE an apPOINTment with you.

4. LET'S turn OFF the AIR conditioner.

5. WHAT'S the PROBlem?

B: Rising Intonation

Example: Did you LOSE the KEYS?

6. Did you HAVE a GOOD TRIP?

7. Have you apPLIED for a CHECK Card?

8. Could I MAKE an apPOINTment with you?

9. Did she turn OFF the AIR conditioner?

10. Is there a PROBlem?

With a partner, take turns saying each sentence. Nod your head slightly as you say the focus word.

Rule 8-2

✔ *If information is new or just introduced, focus shifts to the new piece of information. The previously mentioned information is backgrounded.*

Examples: "Let's conTINue our disCUSsion of polLUtion. / YESterday we deFINED

polLUtion. / ToDAY we'll TALK about the IMpact of polLUtion."

X: WHAT'S your FAVorite desSERT?

Y: ICE cream . . . CHOColate ICE cream.

Information that is implied by the context is usually backgrounded.

Example: I have some ERrands to RUN . . . / and a compoSItion to WRITE.
("to run" and "to write" are understood by the listener)

Exercise 2

Predict the focus word in each utterance and put a dot (•) over it. Then listen to the speakers on tape and check your predictions. Practice the dialogues with a partner.

Example: X: Ouch! Something just stung me!

Y: Was it a bee?

X: It was too big to be a bee. I think it was a hornet.

1. *Dialogue: DEADLINES*

X: What's the matter?

Y: I'm having trouble with this assignment.

X: What kind of assignment?

Y: It's a paper. A philosophy paper. And it's due tomorrow.*

2. *Dialogue: LOST AND FOUND*

X: Look at these sunglasses. Aren't they great?

Y: Where did you get those sunglasses?

X: I found them.

Y: I think those are my sunglasses.

---

*Final time adverbials like *today* and *yesterday* are usually not prominent unless time is the focus:

What're you going to do today?   (activity is the focus of the statement)

My paper's due today.   (time is the focus of the statement)

3. *Dialogue: THE PARTY*

X: When's the party?

Y: Which party?

X: The staff party.

Y: It's Tuesday night.

X: But there's a meeting on Tuesday night.

Y: No. That's been postponed.

4. *Monologue: OPENING A PRESENT*

X: This feels like a book. I love books. It is a book.

5. *Monologue: WHAT'S FOR DINNER?*

X: Uh-oh. It smells like spinach. I hate spinach. Oh, no. It is spinach.

Did you use falling or rising intonation to mark the focus words? Why?

With a partner, choose one dialogue. Modify it in any way you would like. Mark the focus words. Practice the dialogue until you can say it without reading it.

Rule 8-3

☑ *Use focus to highlight contrasts. Contrasts may have more than one major pitch movement in a statement.*

Example (contrast within a statement):

I HAVE some BAD NEWS and some GOOD NEWS.

Example (contrast between statements):

Customer X: I'd LIKE a LARGE ICED TEA.

Customer Y: And I'll have a MEDium ICED TEA.

Sometimes speakers use an extra high pitch to emphasize a contrast.

Example: I went to ROME, GEORgia, but Jean went to ROME, ITaly.

Exercise 3

With a partner, put a dot (•) above the most prominent element(s) in these contrasts. Say each sentence.

Then listen to your teacher or the speakers on tape read the sentences. Compare your predictions.

Example: I'm looking for a used car, / not a new one.

1. This isn't the twenty-fifth floor; / it's the twenty-sixth floor.

2. He found his wallet, / but he never found his credit cards.

3. We'd like to move from the smoking section / to the nonsmoking section.

4. I made the check out to John Nelson / instead of Joan Nelson.

5. I thought our anniversary was on the fourteenth, / but it's on the fifteenth.

Say the sentences with your partner. High-five your partner on the prominent syllables.

Rule 8-4

✔ *Use focus to correct, contradict, or modify a previous statement.*

Example: X: Class is over at four-thirty.

Y: Oh, I thought it was over at five-thirty.

Sometimes new, contrasted, or modified elements occur in syllables or function words that are not ordinarily stressed.

Examples: X: It was nice to meet you.

Y: Nice to meet you.

X: Can we fix the old fax machine?

Y: Ahmed thinks it's possible. I think it's impossible.

Exercise 4

With a partner, correct the statements. Practice the incorrect and correct statements and monitor your partner's use of focus. Try incorporating these expressions:

Are you sure? I thought . . .	*I always thought . . .*
I'm not sure that's right . . .	*I was under the impression . . .*
I don't think so . . .	*I'm almost certain that . . .*
Actually . . .	

Example: INCORRECT: In the United States, you have to be eighTEEN to DRIVE.

CORRECT: I always thought . . . you had to be SIXteen (to DRIVE).*

1. Dante wrote *Hamlet.*

2. Smoking decreases your risk of heart disease.

*Information in parentheses may or may not be expressed.

3. The Taj Mahal is in Thailand.

4. Ecology is the study of personality.

5. The Amazon River is the longest river in the world.

6. CO_2 is the chemical symbol for water.

7. The Atlantic Ocean is to the west of the United States.

8. Kyoto is the capital of Japan.

9. Monet was a famous Dutch painter.

10. George Washington was the second president of the United States.

Listen to the suggested corrections on tape.

Exercise 5

Say each question and response with the speakers on tape or practice with a partner as follows. Student 1 should cover the responses and ask question **a** or **b**. Student 2 should cover the questions and respond with the correct focus.

QUESTIONS (STUDENT 1)	RESPONSES (STUDENT 2)
Examples:	
a. What did you do last night?	I called my mother.
b. You should call your mother.	I called my mother.
a. You look relaxed.	I just got back from a long vacation.
b. You need a long vacation.	I just got back from a long vacation.
1. a. How about a large cheese pizza?	Let's get a medium cheese pizza.
b. How about a medium mushroom pizza?	Let's get a medium cheese pizza.
2. a. Did you sprain your wrist?	I sprained my ankle.
b. Did you break your ankle?	I sprained my ankle.
3. a. Did John ever fax that memo?	No, I faxed it.
b. Did you ever mail that memo?	No, I faxed it.
4. a. Did you say 4×3?	I said $4 + 3$.
b. Did you say $5 + 3$?	I said $4 + 3$.
5. a. Was she a professor at UCLA?	She was a student.
b. Is she a student at UCLA?	She was a student.

PRIME-TIME PRACTICE

Audiotaped Activity: In the early 1900s, the American humorist Mark Twain said, "It is better to give than receive—especially advice." If you had the opportunity to address an audience of high school or college graduates, what advice would you offer? Compose a one-minute "Guide to Life for Graduates" containing three pieces of advice you would share. Mark the prominent element in each sentence or thought group. Record your mini-speech. Listen to your tape and monitor for focus.

Example: Here is a passage from an address Mark Twain gave at a girls'

school in Maryland in 1909: *"There are three things which I consider*
                                                    •
excellent advice. First, don't smoke to excess. Second, don't drink to
                  •   •   •
excess. Third, don't marry to excess."
          •

Suggestion: Read the famous newspaper column "Guide to Life for Graduates" by Mary Schmich at the http://chicagotribune.com Web site.

Rule 8-5

☑ *Use sentence focus to emphasize agreement.*

                    •
Example: X: THIS CHAPter's EAsy.

                         •
             Y: You're RIGHT. It IS EAsy.

When expressing agreement, speakers frequently make an exception to basic rhythm patterns by stressing the verb *to be*, the auxiliary, or *do, does,* or *did.*

                              •
Examples: X: It's been a WARM WINter.

                         •
              Y: It HAS (been a WARM WINter).

                         •
              X: KEN STUdies HARD.

                         •
              Y: He DOES (STUdy HARD).

Exercise 6

In groups of three, use focus to agree or disagree. Student 1 expresses an opinion. Students 2 and 3 close their books and respond by agreeing or disagreeing. Responses should be truthful.

Example: *Student 1:* I think that . . . the Hyundai is the best car on the road.

          Student 2: I agree. It is (the best car on the road).

          Student 3: I think that Toyota's the best (car on the road).

Student 1: I think that . . .

1. Paris is the most beautiful city in the world.

2. Everyone should have three-day weekends.

3. Writing English is easier than speaking it.

4. Guns should be illegal.

5. *Star Wars* is the best movie ever made.

6. Your opinion on a topic: _____

A HELPFUL HINT

When a piece of information is especially important, there are several ways, in addition to focus, to draw a listener's attention to it. To highlight an important word or a key term:

  1. Say it slowly.

  2. Say it softly.

  3. Paraphrase it.

  4. Repeat it.

  5. Use an introductory phrase (e.g., The point is . . .; The bottom line is . . .; The crucial point is . . .).

  6. Emphasize it with upper body movement, a hand or arm gesture, or a head nod.

In the next activity, you will practice using movement.

Exercise 7

Use sentence focus to make inferences. Imagine that you have just entered a room in the middle of a discussion or meeting and that you hear one of the statements on the next page. With a partner, guess a statement that might have *preceded* the one you hear.

Practice saying the "preceding statements" and "statements" with your partner. Use upper body movement (raised eyebrow, hand or arm gesture, head nod) in conjunction with the focus word.

Example: Preceding Statement: _____ *This plan has a lot of advantages.* _____

        Statement: I'm afraid I see some DISadvantages.

1. Preceding Statement: _____

        Statement: Are you sure? Maybe we need TWO new PCs.

2. Preceding Statement: _____

        Statement: I went to the lab on Saturday AND Sunday.

3. Preceding Statement: _____

        Statement: I agree. That IS an unrealistic deadline.

4. Preceding Statement: _____

        Statement: Frank, could YOU do the presentation?

5. Preceding Statement: _____

        Statement: No, the exam is on the FIFTH.

Select one of the dialogues above and present it to your class.

Communicative Practice:
Announcing Schedule Changes

InfoGap

Imagine that you have volunteered to assist with international student orientation at your school and that you must announce a few schedule changes on page 145. Silently rehearse what you will say and then announce the changes to your partner. Highlight the changes with pitch movement and length. Your partner should mark the changes on the schedule on page 146.

    You might begin by saying, "Good morning. Before we get started today, I have some last-minute schedule changes to call to your attention. First of all . . ."

Extend Your Skills . . . to a Contrastive Analysis

You compare and contrast many times a day at home, at work, and at school. You might need to weigh the merits of one university over another, the purchase of one piece of equipment over another, or the choice of one vacation spot over another.

CONTRASTIVE ANALYSIS: With a partner, contrast assumptions about classrooms in the United States versus classrooms in many other countries. One student has chart A on page 147. The other student has chart B on page 148. Complete the charts by sharing information orally. Do not look at your partner's chart. Remember to highlight contrasts.

Example: Student A: In many countries, teachers tend to be FORmal.

Student B: In the United States, teachers tend to be INformal.

Discuss: In groups of three to five students, compare and contrast characteristics of classrooms in your countries.

Oral Review: Intonation and Focus in Discourse

Schedule an individual consultation with your teacher, complete the review as a pair project, or submit the review on tape.

DIRECTIONS: Mark the prominent element or focus in each thought group. Record yourself reading the quotes.

WORDS OF WISDOM

1. We see things not as they are; / we see them as we are.   —Anaïs Nin

2. Whoever gossips to you / will gossip about you.   —Anonymous

3. We will meet your physical force / with soul force.   —Martin Luther King, Jr.

4. We can do no great things; / only small things with great love.   —Mother Teresa

5. The earth does not belong to man. / Man belongs to the earth.   —Chief Seattle

6. Everybody wants to be Cary Grant. / Even I want to be Cary Grant.
—Cary Grant

7. That's one small step for a man, / one giant leap for mankind.
—Neil Armstrong, stepping onto the surface of the moon

8. Genius is one percent inspiration / and ninety-nine percent perspiration.
—Thomas Edison

9. A pessimist thinks the glass is half-empty; / an optimist thinks the glass is half-full.   —Anonymous

10. Ask not what your country can do for you; / ask what you can do for your country.   —John F. Kennedy

Listen to your tape before you submit it. Did you highlight the focus words? Make corrections at the end of your tape.

BEYOND THE PRONUNCIATION CLASSROOM

Comparing Business Practices

Pronunciation Point: Focus to highlight contrasts

Task: With one or more native English speakers, compare business practices in the United States with those in your country.

Before: Fill in the chart with information about work/business customs of your country. Predict a few similarities and/or differences that might exist between the customs in your country and those in the United States.

Area	My Country: _____	United States
Business Cards		
Handshakes		
Gift Giving		
Dress Codes		
Length of Workday		
Length of Workweek		
Vacation Time		

After: Report on your experience to the class. What were the most interesting similarities or differences? Use focus to highlight contrasts.

More Functions of Intonation

Intonation is the rise and fall in the pitch of the voice. In Chapter 8, you learned how intonation signals the focus words in statements and questions. In this chapter, you will learn more functions of intonation.

You'll learn how intonation changes a statement of fact . . .

He CLOSED his CHECKing account.

to an expression of uncertainty . . .

He CLOSED his CHECKing account?

You'll learn how intonation changes a request for information . . .

WHOM is she MARrying?

to a request for clarification . . .

WHOM is she MARrying?

You will also learn about intonation patterns that signal a choice . . .

I'm TAKing biOLogy or CHEMistry.

and patterns that signal items in a series . . .

I'm TAKing biOLogy, SPANish, and P.E.

Listen!

Listening Activity

What are the intonation patterns in the following sentences? Listen to the speaker on tape or ask a native English speaker to say the sentences. Draw ↘ or ↗ over the prominent word (or syllable) with a major pitch fall or pitch rise in each thought group.

Example: We can take a cab / or a bus.

1. Would you rather live in a dorm / or an apartment?

2. X: You look busy.

   Y: I am. / I'm not sure if I'm coming / or going.

3. Which do you want first— / the bad news / or the good news?

4. Should we leave a tip of fifteen percent / or twenty percent?

5. X: Could I get my grade?

   Y: Which grade—/ your exam grade / or your course grade?

6. X: What would you like on your sandwich?

   Y: I'll have mustard, / lettuce, / tomato, / and pickles.

7. Intonation patterns can convey emotions like excitement, / irritation, / and disappointment.

8. X: The area code is 202.

   Y: 202?

9. It's time to eat, / Mr. Baker.

10. There's a place to park, / Dr. Sitter.

Compare your answers with those of the other members of the class.

Note about rising intonation: Sometimes speakers use a fall-rise instead of just a rise.

Example: Could I get my grade? (or) Could I get my grade?

Rules and Practices

Some intonation patterns express attitudes and emotions like anger, doubt, irony, and sarcasm. These patterns are variable and difficult to learn. Other intonation patterns are essential for giving information and participating in discussions and conversations.

Rule 9-1

Listen to this example of a sentence that presents a choice. How do you know a choice is being offered?

Example: Do you want paper or plastic?

✔ ***In a statement or a question that presents a choice, the first alternative has a rising pitch and the second has a falling pitch.***

Examples: Is the exam today or tomorrow?

   To be / or not to be.

Exercise 1

Say these sentences with your teacher or the speaker on tape. Then write three original sentences that present choices. These should be sentences you would be likely to say. With a partner, take turns saying all the sentences.

1. Was the light yellow or red?

2. Is the speed limit 65 or 70?

3. You should walk on the sidewalk or on the shoulder.

4. Should we take your car or mine?

5. Signal a turn with your blinker or your hand.

6. Should I turn left or right?

7. Would you rather walk or ride?

8. _____

9. _____

10. _____

PRIME-TIME PRACTICE

Reading Poetry: The well-known poem "Dream Deferred," by Langston Hughes, asks the reader to consider alternatives. Read the poem for meaning.

Step 1: Mark the poem with ➚ and ➘ pitch marks over the focus words. Rehearse the poem, silently or out loud.

Step 2: Record yourself reading the poem. Then rewind your tape and monitor for pitch movement on the focus words.

Step 3: Record a one-minute response. What do you think happens to a dream deferred? Submit the tape to the teacher.

Step 4: In the next class, do a round-robin reading of the poem.

Dream Deferred

What happens to a dream
deferred?

Does it dry up
like a raisin in the sun?

Or fester like a sore—
And then run?

Does it stink like rotten meat?
Or crust and sugar over—
like a syrupy sweet?

Maybe it just sags
like a heavy load.

Or does it explode?

Rule 9-2

Listen to items in a series. How do you know that more items are on the list? How do you know when the speaker has reached the last item?

Example: I lost my keys, my wallet, and my passport.

☑ *When you list two or more items in a series, the pitch rises on the stressed syllable of every item except the last. The rise signals "more to come"; the fall signals "the end."*

Example: While you're at the store, please get dog food, coffee filters, and chicken wings.

Exercise 2

With a partner, take turns saying the sentences. Monitor your partner's intonation.

1. The Environmental Protection Agency (EPA) protects the air, soil, and water.

2. If I get a new PC, I'll need a table, a printer, and some speakers.

3. Grades are based on class participation, two papers, and three exams.

4. The fringe benefits include two weeks' paid vacation, six paid holidays, and health insurance.

5. The apartment has a kitchen, a living room, two bedrooms, and a bath.

Exercise 3

Items in a series can be words, phrases, or even clauses. In small groups, choose one situation below and create a response. Then give your response orally to the class.

Situation a. You have been working on a report for the past two weeks. The deadline is today, but the report is not ready because *the computers were down last week, someone who has vital information has been out of town, and you have been sick.* In a diplomatic way, ask for an extension and give three good reasons why the extension is justified.

Your request with three good reasons: _____

_____

Situation b. It is Saturday afternoon. Your 12-year-old son wants to go to a movie with a friend. However, he neglected his chores for the week (*taking out the garbage, feeding the dog, and cutting the grass*) and his room is a mess. Tell your son what he must do before he goes to the movie.

Reply with three or four conditions: _____

_____

Situation c. You work for an engineering firm. You are preparing a technical presentation on heat transfer for clients with no technical background. You will explain the three ways heat energy can be transferred from one place to another: *conduction, convection, and radiation.* Give a brief introduction and introduce the three methods.

Introduction with the three major subtopics: _____

_____

Rule 9-3

In this example, how does speaker Y indicate surprise?

Example: X: He has 10 brothers.

　　　　　Y: He has 10 brothers? (I'm really surprised.)

✔ ***You can show surprise or disbelief by using rising pitch to echo a statement. The pitch rise is usually on the stressed syllable of the last content word.***

Example: X: She's a grandmother.

　　　　　Y: She's a grandmother? (You're kidding. She looks so young.)

Exercise 4

Say the following dialogues with the speakers on tape or practice them with a partner. Speaker Y should indicate surprise and incorporate one of these introductory expressions:

　　You're kidding . . .   You're joking . . .   You've got to be kidding . . .

　　No way . . .   I don't believe it . . .   You can't be serious . . .   Are you sure? . . .

Example: X: Victor lost his job.

　　　　　Y: You're kidding . . . he lost his job?

1. X: He's majoring in economics.

　　Y: He's majoring in economics? He can't even balance his checkbook.

2. X: I failed statistics.

　　Y: You failed statistics?

3. X: I'm moving to the Pacific Northwest.

　　Y: You're moving to the Pacific Northwest? Why?

4. X: Carl totaled his car.

　　Y: He totaled his car? Was he hurt?

5. X: Ms. Brown's out of town.

　　Y: She's out of town?

Rule 9-4

 Listen to the intonation pattern for requesting clarification or more information. It is similar to the pattern for surprise.

☑ *If you want clarification of the entire statement, the pitch rises on the last content word.*

Example: X: I broke my leg.

Y: You broke your leg? (How did you do that?)

☑ *If you want clarification or repetition of a specific item, the pitch rises on the specific item you want clarified.*

Example: X: The number is 555-2435.

Y: 555-2435? (I'm not certain of the fourth number.)

Exercise 5

Say these dialogues with the speakers on tape or practice with a partner. Speaker X makes a statement. Speaker Y responds, raising his or her pitch (and eyebrows!) on the item to be clarified.

Example: X: I'll meet you at 5:45.

Y: At 9:45?

X: No. At 5:45.

1. X: My e-mail is jdoe@univ.edu.

Y: jtoe?

X: No. "D" as in "dog."

2. X: We'll all meet behind Candler Hall.

Y: Behind Candler Hall?

X: That's right.

3. X: The cheapest one-way fare is $1,500.

Y: One-way fare?

X: I'm sorry. I mean round-trip.

Rule 9-5

Listen to these two dialogues. Why did Speaker X answer the same question in two different ways?

Dialogue 1: X: I'm going to the Middle East.
     Y: Where?
     X: Lebanon.

Dialogue 2: X: I'm going to the Middle East.
     Y: Where?
     X: The Middle East.

✔ *In a wh-question, if the pitch falls, the speaker is probably seeking more information. If the pitch rises, the speaker is probably requesting repetition or clarification. When seeking repetition, the pitch rise occurs on the wh-word.*

Exercise 6

In this practice, Student 1 makes a statement. Student 2 responds with a *wh*-word with either a rising or falling intonation. Student 1 then chooses the correct response. Switch roles and repeat.

Example: STUDENT 1 (X): I'm going to Brazil.

    STUDENT 2 (Y): Where? (or) Where?

    STUDENT 1 (X): Brazil. (or) Rio.

1. X: They moved their headquarters near campus.

 Y: Where?   (or) Where?

 X: Near campus. (or) On 10th Street.

2. X: I left my umbrella on the bus.

 Y: Where?   (or) Where?

 X: On the bus.   (or) On the front seat.

3. X: The next game is this weekend.

 Y: When?   (or) When?

 X: This weekend. (or) On Saturday.

4. X: I'll call you in the morning.

 Y: When?   (or) When?

 X: In the morning. (or) About 9:00.

5. X: There was a terrible earthquake in Turkey.

 Y: Where?   (or) Where?

 X: In Turkey.   (or) Istanbul.

Rule 9-6

Listen to these examples of direct address.

Examples: They've already left, Mr. Johnson.

Did they leave, Mr. Johnson?

✔ ***When you use direct address at the end of a sentence, a person's name is usually spoken as a separate phrase that starts low and rises slightly.***

Example: What did you buy, Mary?

Exercise 7

Listen as your teacher or the speaker on tape reads sentence a or b. Circle the one you hear.

Example: **a.** Are you bathing children? (One focus word; children are being spoken *about*)

b. Are you bathing, children? (Two focus words; children are being spoken *to*)

1. a. We have to pay John.

b. We have to pay, John.

2. a. I don't understand Dr. White.

b. I don't understand, Dr. White.

3. a. Are you hiring Jane?

b. Are you hiring, Jane?

4. a. I need to see Dr. White.

b. I need to see, Dr. White.

5. a. I didn't call Lee.

b. I didn't call, Lee.

Check your answers with your teacher. With a partner, practice saying the circled sentences.

Write three short sentences with direct address. Use the names of people you know and titles if appropriate. Dictate your sentences to your partner.

1. _____

2. _____

3. _____

Exercise 8

With a partner, mark the following dialogue for sentence focus and for rising and falling pitch patterns. Practice the dialogue with the speakers on tape or practice in groups of three students sitting in a circle. Switch roles and practice it again.

ORDERING BEVERAGES

WAITER: What would you like to drink, Sir?

PATRON A: Just water.

WAITER: And what would you like to drink?

PATRON B: I'll have tea.

WAITER: Hot or iced?

PATRON B: Iced.

WAITER: Sweetened or unsweetened?

PATRON B: Uh . . . unsweetened.

WAITER: Do you want that now or with your meal?

PATRON B: You can bring it now.

SOMETHING TO THINK ABOUT

The more senses you activate in pronunciation practice, the more likely conscious patterns will become automatic. This text links your pronunciation practice with vision, listening, and movement so that new patterns will gradually become a part of your long-term memory.

Communicative Practice: Mini-Dramas

You and your partner will develop dialogue for one of the three situations below. Student 1 should read Role X on page 149, and Student 2 should read Role Y on page 150 for the same situation. Without looking at each other's role descriptions, take a few minutes to create an impromptu dialogue beginning with Role X. Practice your dialogue until it is smooth and natural. Incorporate appropriate movement and gesture. Present your mini-drama to the class.

Extend Your Skills . . . to Interviews and Surveys

Interview your classmates about the most important technological innovations of the 20th century.

Step 1: Review the word stress patterns in the inventions below.

Step 2: Work in pairs. A interviews B while C interviews D. Then reverse roles: B interviews A, and D interviews C. Follow up questions on the chart with clarification questions (e.g., "The computer has been more beneficial than antibiotics?").

Step 3: In small groups, report what you learned from your partner. One person in the group should keep a written record. What were the most frequently mentioned innovations?

Inventions of the 20th Century	Which innovation has affected your daily life the most? How?	Which innovation has been the most beneficial to humankind? How?	What do you wish had not been invented? Why?	Total
MIcrowave OVen				
WASHing machine				
ComPUter				
AUtomobile				
TELevision				
ReFRIGerator				
AntibiOTics				
AIRplane/ SPACE flight				
INternet				
NUclear WEApons				
CREdit card				
GeNETic engiNEERing				

Oral Review: More Functions of Intonation

Name: _____ Date: _____

Schedule an individual consultation with your teacher, complete the review as a group project, or submit the review on tape.

Part A

Read the following short dialogues with a partner. If you complete this segment on tape, ask a roommate, spouse, or friend to read one of the parts.

1. X: What was your major, Ali?

    Y: Graduate or undergraduate?

2. X: Where are you going, Maria?

    Y: I'm going to the bank, the dentist, and the mall.

3. X: How many people did Sara invite to her wedding?

    Y: Eighty.

    X: How many?

    Y: Eighty.

Part B

Refer to the technological innovations survey in this chapter. In your opinion, what are the three most important technological innovations of the 20th century? Present them in the form of a list and use intonation for items in a series. Then briefly explain your reasons for choosing each one.

Listen to your tape before you submit it. Make any corrections at the end of the tape.

BEYOND THE PRONUNCIATION CLASSROOM

Placing a Food Order

Pronunciation Focus: Intonation in questions and items in a series.

Task: Call a restaurant to place a food order for you and your friends or family for pick-up or delivery.

Before: Bring carry-out menus to class. Think about what you might order and the interaction that might occur. With a partner, rehearse what you might say, paying special attention to intonation. Practice giving directions to the delivery person.

Sample Utterances with Intonation Patterns:

Do you have any specials?

I'll have a large cheese pizza, a large Greek salad, and

an order of breadsticks.

What's the total?

Do you deliver, or do I have to pick it up?

After: Discuss your experience with your classmates. Try to re-create as much of the actual dialogue as you can. Analyze the intonation patterns of the dialogue.

Phrasing, Pausing, and Linking

Speakers of English organize words into short, meaningful groups of words. Each of these groups has a major focus and is called a *thought group.* If speakers do not divide the stream of speech into thought groups, listeners have difficulty understanding, no matter how clearly each word is pronounced.

Languages signal thought groups in different ways. In English, speakers use intonation—a pitch fall or rise—to mark the end of a thought group. The pitch fall or rise is sometimes accompanied by a brief pause.

The information below is organized into thought groups to make it easier to understand. Thought groups are separated with a slash (/).

Phone number: 202 / 555 / 1212

Social Security Number: 360 / 42 / 5548

Sentence: In terms of male life expectancy, / the country of Iceland / ranks the highest, / with 74 years.

Within thought groups, English speakers make a smooth connection between words by linking the final sound of one word with the beginning sound of the next word. As a result, words within a thought group often sound like one long word. It is sometimes difficult to hear where one word ends and the next word begins.

Notice the smooth transition between words in these very short sentences.

This is easy.

Is Ed there?

In this chapter, you'll practice delivering information in meaningful thought groups and making smooth transitions between words in thought groups.

Listen!

Listening Activity 1

Listen to your teacher or the speaker on tape say the phrases. If you hear one thought group, circle *a.* If you hear two thought groups, circle *b.*

1. **a.** twenty-seven-foot basketball players

   b. twenty / seven-foot basketball players

2. **a.** forty-eight-foot boards

   b. forty / eight-foot boards

3. a. twenty-nine-cent stamps

   b. twenty / nine-cent stamps

4. a. eighty-five-foot women

   b. eighty / five-foot women

5. a. seven-week-long vacations

   b. seven / week-long vacations

6. a. three-hour-long tests

   b. three / hour-long tests

Check your answers with your teacher. With your class, discuss how thought groups change the meanings of the phrase pairs.

Listening Activity 2

Listen to your teacher or the speaker on tape read this transcript of a radio advertisement two times. The first time, listen for meaning. The second time, indicate with a slash (/) the slight pitch fall marking the end of each thought group.

> "Unlike other copier companies, Mita doesn't make cameras, or televisions, or calculators, or videocassette recorders, or bicycles, or telephone answering machines, or car stereos, or vacuum cleaners, or movies, watches, Scotch recording tape, batteries, or film. The fact is, Mita doesn't make anything but great copiers. After all, we didn't get to be the fastest growing copier company for the last five years by selling microwave ovens. Mita. All we make are great copiers."

Compare your answers with those of the rest of the class. What was the average number of words in the thought groups?

A HELPFUL HINT

How do you know if it is your turn to speak? Intonation offers some clues. If you hear a deep or **full pitch fall** at the end of a thought group, it is probably a final thought group. The speaker is probably finished with his or her statement or turn.

Example: I can't see.

If you hear a **half pitch fall** at the end of a thought group, it is probably a nonfinal thought group. The speaker probably wishes to complete the message or to hold the floor. Sometimes speakers follow the half fall with a slight rise to indicate "more to come."

Example: I can't see / paying that much for a car. (or)

I can't see / paying that much for a car.

Listening Activity 3

Listen to the half pitch fall marking nonfinal thought groups and the full pitch fall marking final thought groups. Your teacher or the speakers on tape will say the statements and responses below. Circle response *a* if the speaker seems to be finished. Circle response *b* if the speaker seems to have more to say.

1. What did your teacher do after class?

    a. He passed out.

    b. He passed out . . . (our exam grades.)

2. Did you register for biology?

    a. No. I registered for chemistry.

    b. No. I registered for chemistry . . . (because . . .)

3. What did John say?

    a. He said / he doesn't like his children.

    b. He said / he doesn't like his children . . . (going to a school like that.)

4. John has a new part-time job.

    a. But he doesn't want it.

    b. But he doesn't want it . . . (to affect his studies.)

5. Could you give me your credit card number please?

    a. 4307 / 3198 / 4010

    b. 4307 / 3198 / 4010 . . . (8238)

Rules and Practices 1:
Phrases and Thought Groups

Writers make ideas clear to readers by using commas, periods, and indented paragraphs. Speakers make ideas clear to listeners by using thought groups.

Woman without her man / is helpless.

Woman / without her / man is helpless.

Decisions about where thought groups begin and end vary from speaker to speaker and from situation to situation. Informal speech has longer thought groups and fewer pauses. Formal speech has shorter thought groups and more breaks.

Examples: I'll call you when I get home. (rapid, informal speech)

Please call / if you have to cancel. (slower, more formal speech)

Here are some general guidelines to help you communicate your thoughts more clearly.

Rule 10-1

☑ *The end of a clause is often the end of a thought group. Use a slight drop in pitch and sometimes a brief pause.*

Examples: Whatever you do, / do well.

The phone always rings / when I'm in the shower.

Notice that the slight pitch fall occurs on the focus word or prominent element in each thought group.

Rule 10-2

☑ *The end of a phrase is often the end of a thought group. Use a slight drop in pitch and occasionally a brief pause. Typical thought groups will depend on the length of the phrase and may include prepositional phrases, verb phrases, and noun phrases.*

Example: I leave for work / at six A.M. / every morning.

Rule 10-3

☑ *Transitional or parenthetical expressions (first, finally, of course, on the other hand) form thought groups.*

Example: Our profit margin, / as you all know, / has decreased substantially / this past quarter.

Exercise 1

With a partner, unscramble one job description in section A or B. Organize the thought groups into a logical description and share your description with the class.

Remember that nonfinal thought groups have a slight pitch fall (or fall-rise) on the focus and that final thought groups have a full pitch fall.

Example: Professional philosophers / are employed almost exclusively / by colleges and universities.

Note: Some speakers might add a slight pitch fall after *employed* and after *colleges*.

NOUN PHRASES	VERB PHRASES	PREPOSITIONAL PHRASES
Section A:		
1. Professional philosophers	risk bodily injury	by colleges and universities
2. Most firefighters	advise clients	in their calculations
3. NFL players	must be accurate	about their hair
4. Nuclear engineers	usually travel	by fire and smoke
5. Licensed cosmetologists	are employed almost exclusively	on chartered jets
Section B:		
6. School principals	are occasionally invited	with rude and demanding people
7. Travel agents	must express their thoughts	at all times of the day and night
8. Writers of books	are on call	in group practices
9. Some secretaries	work together	in a precise manner
10. Nuclear plant decontamination experts	are forced to interact	on promotional cruises
11. A large majority of doctors	are always dealing	with disciplinary problems

After each pair presents its description to the class, "walk each sentence." Step on the focus of each thought group. Then stand still and say the sentence one more time.

Exercise 2

In each sentence, the thought group in parentheses is misplaced. Indicate its correct position in the sentence with a ∧ .

Say the corrected sentences with the speaker on tape. Or take turns saying the sentences with a partner. Divide the long sentences into thought groups.

Examples: The hostess served the dinner ∧ to her guests (that she had been warming in the oven).

Please take time ∧ to look over the brochure that is enclosed (with your family).

1. A calf was born to a farmer (with two heads).

2. The Toyota hit a utility pole (going about 45 miles per hour).

3. The patient was referred to a psychiatrist (with a severe emotional problem).

4. She died in the home in which she was born (at the age of 88).

5. Here are some suggestions for handling obscene phone calls (from the New England Telephone Company).

PRIME-TIME PRACTICE

Audiotaped Activity

Step 1: Read the political anecdotes below. Mark thought groups with slashes (/). Mark the focus of each thought group with a dot (•).

Step 2: Rehearse the stories.

Step 3: Record yourself (a) reading the stories and (b) telling the stories in your own words.

Step 4: Listen to the recording and monitor for thought groups. Did you make it easy for the listener to comprehend each thought group?

Step 5: Submit the tape to your teacher for feedback.

Anecdote 1:

U.S. President Calvin Coolidge was known as a man of few words. At a reception one evening, a woman told him, "Mr. President, I have a bet with a friend that I can get more than three words out of you tonight." The president turned to her and said, "You lose."

Anecdote 2:

The British Prime Minister Winston Churchill was a frequent dinner guest at the White House. At a dinner one evening, a woman seated next to Churchill kept complaining about his policies. She told him, "If I were your wife, I would give you poison." He replied, "If I were your husband, I would take it."

*Sentences 2–5 from Richard Lederer, *Anguished English* (New York: Laurel, 1987), pp. 150–154.
Copyright Wyrick & Company. Reprinted by permission.

Exercise 3

The following excerpt is from an August 1969 interview with astronaut Michael Collins after the Apollo 11 flight to the moon. Imagine dividing each of the very long sentences into several small packages or thought groups. Mark the sentences with slashes (/) for thought groups. Mark the focus of each thought group with a dot (•).

With a partner, compare your thought groups. Practice the question-answer exchange.

REPORTER: "I'm struck from the movies and the still pictures by the difference in the very hostile appearance of the moon when you're orbiting over it or some distance from it and the warmer colors and the relatively apparently more friendly appearance of it when you're on the surface. I'd like to ask Colonel Collins if he gets that same impression from the pictures . . ."

COLLINS: "The moon changes character as the angle of the sunlight striking its surface changes. At very low sun angles close to the terminator at dawn or dusk, it has the harsh, forbidding characteristics which you see in a lot of the photographs.

On the other hand, when the sun is more closely overhead, the midday situation, the moon takes on more of a brown color. It becomes almost a rosy looking place— a fairly friendly place so that from dawn through midday through dusk you run the whole gamut. It starts off very forbidding, becomes friendly, and then becomes forbidding again as the sun disappears."*

*From *The First Lunar Landing as Told by the Astronauts, 20th Anniversary*, National Aeronautics and Space Administration, Office of Public Affairs, 1989, p. 21.

Rules and Practices 2: Linking

In rapid speech, when one word is linked with the next, sounds cluster together. Some sounds are lost, some are added, some shift to different words, some change, and some are spoken almost simultaneously.

Most sound changes are too complex to learn consciously, but many of these changes will occur automatically if you make an effort to blend or link together words in the same thought group.

A few of the more useful rules for linking follow. These guidelines will help not only your pronunciation but also your comprehension of native speaker speech.

Rule 10-4

☑ *When consecutive words in the same thought group end and begin with the same consonant sound, the sound is held or lengthened, not pronounced twice.*

Examples:	at_twelve	(hold *t*)
	big_game	(hold *g*)
	good_deal	(hold *d*)
	class_schedule	(lengthen *s*)
	he'll_look	(lengthen *l*)
	with_three	(lengthen *th*)

☑ *When consecutive words in the same thought group end and begin with similar consonants (made in the same part of the mouth), combine the two sounds into one.*

Examples: late_dinner

help_me

bought_some

sit_down

fat_chance

Rule 10-5

☑ *When a word begins with a vowel sound, borrow the final consonant sound from the previous word in the same thought group.*

Examples: pick_it_up   = pi ki tup

take_off   = ta koff

drop_him_off = dro pi moff

Rule 10-6

☑ *Stop consonants—/p/ and /b/, /k/ and /g/, and /t/ and /d/—at the ends of words are spoken at almost the same time as the first consonant sounds in the next words. Hold the stop until you are ready to say the next sound.*

Examples: cab_driver   (hold /b/ until you are ready to say /d/)

lab_technician

stop_sign

keep_trying

lap_top computer

look_like

big_problem

Exercise 4

To practice linking and blending, repeat these phrases after the speaker on tape or your teacher or practice with a partner.

Examples: Cub Scouts   (hold /b/ until you are ready to say /s/)

                   help out   (move the /p/ to the next word)

                   green notebook   (lengthen the /n/)

job training	look tired
job ladder	look sick
job offer	look up
job benefits	look carefully

lab coat	big debt
lab assistant	big meeting
lab equipment	big game
lab procedures	big organization

help teach	got caught
help make	got thirsty
help organize	got tired
help people	got arrested

deep trouble	caused misunderstanding
deep water	caused problems
deep thinker	caused deaths
deep in debt	caused anxiety

Exercise 5

Write the titles of your three favorite films below. Practice saying each movie title as if it were one word. Share your favorite titles with your class.

Examples: Dances with Wolves

                 Sound of Music

                 Sleepless in Seattle

1. _____

2. _____

3. _____

Rule 10-7

Listen to these questions. What sound change do you hear when /t/ is blended with /y/?

Examples: Don't you know?

Haven't you heard?

Can't you go?

☑ ***When a word ends in /t/ and the next word begins with /y/, the blended sound is /t ʃ/ as in choose. This sound combination is common in negative questions.***

Example: Don't you . . .   (sounds like "don chew")

Rule 10-8

What sound change occurs when /d/ is blended with /y/ in these short sentences?

Examples: Did you know?

Would you come?

Could you help?

I called you.

☑ ***When a word ends in /d/ and the next word begins with /y/, the blended sound is /dʒ/ as in juice. This sound combination is common in past tense questions and questions with could, should, and would.***

Example: Did you   (sounds like "di joo")

Could you (sounds like "cou joo")

Communicative Practice: Driving Test

Use thought groups and blending as you give your partner an oral driving test.

One partner should mark questions 1 through 6 on page 151 for thought groups (/) and linking. The other partner should mark questions 7 through 12 on page 152. Practice the questions until the thought groups sound natural and the blending is smooth. Ask your partner the questions you marked. Write your partner's answers.

Preview blending in these thought groups:

. . . should you walk on   . . . set your headlights

. . . if you start to skid   . . . should you exchange

. . . should you use   . . . what should you do

. . . how should you

Compare your answers with your classmates'. Driving laws vary from state to state. Consult the driver's manual for your state if you are unsure of an answer.

A HELPFUL HINT

In spontaneous speech, speakers of American English frequently hesitate while planning what they are going to say or while searching for a word they need. These hesitations, if not excessive, are a normal part of spontaneous speech. Most native speakers never eliminate hesitations in their speech, and you probably won't either.

If you need to hesitate to plan or think, be sure the pause or silent period is brief. If you wish to hold the floor while you are thinking, use fillers or hesitation devices.

You can use fillers **within** thought groups . . .

> *Example*: Can you hand me / the ***uuuhhhh*** stapler.

. . . or **between** thought groups.

> *Example*: My ID number is / ***I'm not sure*** / ***let's see*** / IV 68.

PEANUTS © United Feature Syndicate
Reprinted by Permission.

Extend Your Skills . . . to a Process Presentation

Explain an interesting process from sports, your daily life, or your field of work or study. Choose a process that has at least three distinct steps and that can be explained clearly in about two minutes (e.g., how to eat Japanese noodles, how to make a perfect bowl of popcorn, how to fall asleep quickly).

The presentation will provide an opportunity to use all the skills learned in this course; however, the primary purpose of the explanation is to practice the following:

1. Transition words like *first, next, after that,* and *finally* to signal each step of the process

2. Signal words like *for example, in other words,* and *to say it another way* to clarify and rephrase important information in your presentation

3. Pitch fall and pause to mark thought groups, especially to set off transition words and rephrased information

4. Brief pauses to set off major segments of your presentation (between each step in your process)

Outline your presentation. For each step in your process, tell the audience *what* the step is, *why* it is important, and *how* you accomplish it. Use visual aids (simple outlines, diagrams, pictures, or flow charts) to add interest and clarity.

Rehearse your presentation several times, using only your outline. Use a simple, clear, direct speaking style.

Video- or audiotape your presentation. Self-evaluate the recording on the form that follows. Submit the form to your teacher.

Process Presentation/Self-Evaluation Form

Name: _____   Topic: _____

Scoring Form: Listen to your tape. Assign 1 point for each component below. You may need to listen to your tape several times.

A: Delivery   1 point each

  1. Attention to time limit   _____

  2. Well organized   _____

    — Clear introduction

    — Effective transitions

    — Clear conclusion

  3. Repetition/rephrasing   _____

  4. Interesting   _____

  5. Appropriate level of complexity   _____

                   (Part A) _____ $\times$ 10 = _____

B: Pronunciation/Clarity   1 point each

  1. Clear consonants and vowels
in key words   _____

  2. Good stress in key words   _____

  3. Effective sentence stress and focus   _____

  4. Appropriate thought groups/
pausing   _____

  5. Adequate speed and volume   _____

                   (Part B) _____ $\times$ 10 = _____

                   TOTAL (Part A + B) = _____%

Comments:

_____

_____

_____

_____

_____

_____

_____

Oral Review: Phrasing, Pausing, and Linking

Name: _____ Date: _____

Schedule an individual consultation with your teacher, complete the review as a group project, or submit the review on tape. Finish marking the thought groups and the focus of each thought group below. Record your reading.

What's In a Name?*

•   •   •
Experts say / that what you name your child / can make a huge difference. /

Professor Albert Mehrabian, a psychologist at UCLA, has studied how names affect

the way we think of people. In thousands of interviews, he asked Americans to react

to certain names. Reactions were very similar. The name *Rock,* for example, got top

marks for masculinity but low marks for morals. The name *Prudence* ranked high for

morality but low for cheerfulness. In general, people with long names were perceived

as successful. *Alexander,* for example, ranked high in success for men; *Elizabeth,*

Victoria, and *Olympia* ranked high in success for women. People with short names

like *Amy* and *Jim* were perceived as popular and friendly. The same was true of

nicknames like *Bob* for Robert or *Bill* for William. In general, Dr. Mehrabian advises

parents to choose traditional, popular names for their children.

* Adapted from "The Power of a Name" by Michael Ryan in *Parade Magazine,* September 22, 1996, p. 12.

Listen to your tape before you submit it. Did you use thought groups? Did you link words within thought groups? Make corrections at the end of the tape.

BEYOND THE PRONUNCIATION CLASSROOM

Checking Air Fares

Are you, a friend, or a family member planning a trip by air in the near future?

Pronunciation Point: Thought groups and phrasing

Task: Call the airlines. Make a reservation or simply inquire about the lowest available fares.

Before: How would you communicate the following sample information? Mark logical thought groups. With a partner, predict the interaction and practice delivering the information.

I need to check round-trip fares from _____ to _____.

I'll be departing on _____ at about _____.

My return will be on _____ at about _____.

Name: _____

Number and Street: _____

City, State, and Zip Code: _____

Telephone Number: (_ _ _ _ _ _ _ _ _ _)

Type of Credit Card: _____

Name on Card: _____

Card Number*: (_ _ _ _ _ _ _ _ _ _ _ _ _ _ _ _)

Expiration Date: (_ _ _ _)
                       mo/yr

After: Did you remember to organize your speech into meaningful thought groups? Report on your experience to the class.

*Make up a 16-digit number when practicing.

STOCK LIST A

Items to be ordered:	Currently in Stock	Target Inventory
Computer monitors	24	
Computer keyboards	41	43
Desktop computer systems		29
Business software packages		
TOEFL review books	36	
Art brushes	74	
T-shirts		113
Scientific calculators		
Pairs of sunglasses	0	
Pencil cases	53	
Alarm clocks		230

[Order form is on page 41.]

STOCK LIST B

Items to be ordered:	Currently in Stock	Target Inventory
Computer monitors		37
Computer keyboards		
Desktop computer systems	11	
Business software packages	19	19
TOEFL review books		60
Art brushes		70
T-shirts	113	
Scientific calculators	47	53
Pairs of sunglasses		250
Pencil cases		65
Alarm clocks	193	

[Order form is on page 41.]

Heinle & Heinle Publishers/ITP © 2001 Reproducible

Name:
Account Number 113-980-614-3

No.	Date	Description	Payment	Deposit	Balance
	6/11	Payroll		125.00	430.90
311	6/11	AT&T	26.60		404.30
312	6/12	Stacey's Drugstore	9.15		395.15
313	6/13	Mastercard	45.00		350.15
314	6/15		17.05		333.10
315	6/16	City of Riverdale - traffic court	40.00		293.10
316	6/17	Supercuts - haircut			
	6/18	ATM	50.00		
317	6/19	Check Card - Comp USA	13.10		
		Service charge	5.00		
318	6/19	TWA - Airline ticket	200.00		

National Bank of Illinois (NBI)
2000 Riverside Parkway
Riverdale

Name _____

Account Number 113 980 614 3

-CHECKS POSTED-

DATE	CHECK NUMBER	AMOUNT	BALANCE
06-11	Deposit	125.00	430.90
06-15	311	26.60	404.30
06-16	312	9.15	395.15
06-17	313	45.00	350.15
06-19	314*	17.05	333.10
06-20	315	40.00	293.10
06-21	316	13.00	280.10
06-22	Withdrawal	50.00	230.10
06-23	317	30.10	200.00
06-23	Service Chg.	5.00	195.00
06-23	318	200.00	−5.00

*Check number 314 was written to Cambridge Bookstore for textbooks, according to the canceled check.

KEY TO LOCATION

FIRST FLOOR

A. Circulation (checkout)

B. Periodicals/Foreign Newspapers

C. Rest Rooms

D. Fire Exit

E. Catalogs/Databases

SECOND FLOOR

F. CDs/Cassettes

G. Photography

H. Copy Services

I. Psychology

J. Biography

K. Biological Sciences

THIRD FLOOR

L. Education

M. Anthropology

N. Political Science

O. Cookbooks

P. Mathematics

Q. Engineering

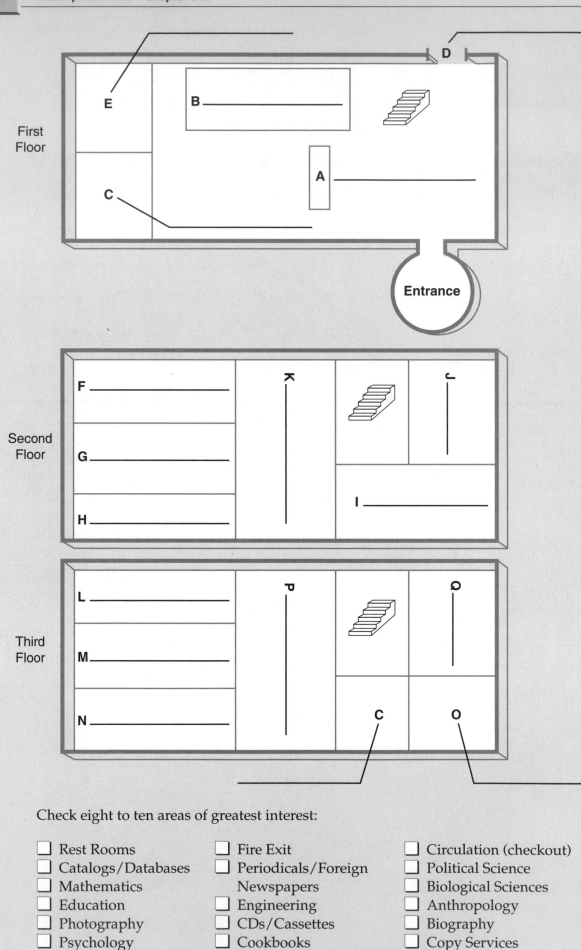

First Floor

Second Floor

Third Floor

Check eight to ten areas of greatest interest:

- [ ] Rest Rooms
- [ ] Catalogs/Databases
- [ ] Mathematics
- [ ] Education
- [ ] Photography
- [ ] Psychology

- [ ] Fire Exit
- [ ] Periodicals/Foreign Newspapers
- [ ] Engineering
- [ ] CDs/Cassettes
- [ ] Cookbooks

- [ ] Circulation (checkout)
- [ ] Political Science
- [ ] Biological Sciences
- [ ] Anthropology
- [ ] Biography
- [ ] Copy Services

Heinle & Heinle Publishers/ITP © 2001 Reproducible

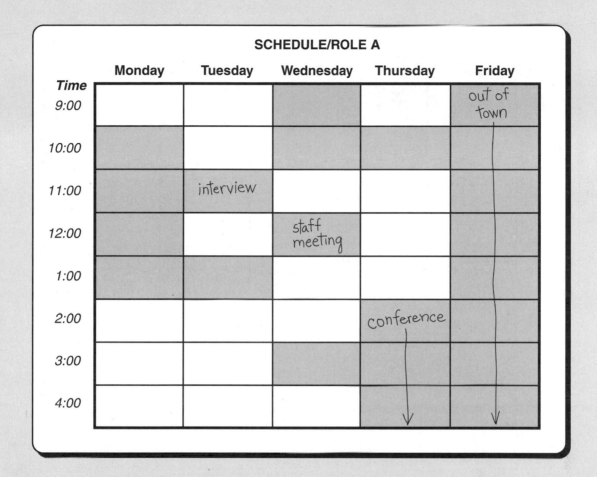

SCHEDULE/ROLE A

Time	Monday	Tuesday	Wednesday	Thursday	Friday
9:00					out of town
10:00					
11:00		interview			
12:00			staff meeting		
1:00					
2:00				conference	
3:00					
4:00					

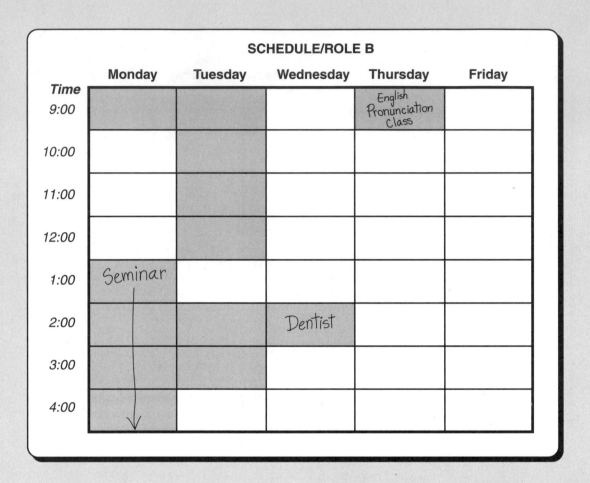

SCHEDULE/ROLE B

Time	Monday	Tuesday	Wednesday	Thursday	Friday
9:00				English Pronunciation Class	
10:00					
11:00					
12:00					
1:00	Seminar				
2:00			Dentist		
3:00					
4:00					

WELCOME TO INTERNATIONAL STUDENT ORIENTATION
August 19

Dean's Welcome | Candler Chapel

9:00–~~9:30~~ 9:20

Immigration Sessions | Student Center, Room ~~213~~ 313, F-1 Visa Holders

9:30–10:30 | Student Center, Room 355, J-1 Visa Holders

Refreshment Break, Commons
10:30-10:45

Health Care in the U.S. | Student Center, Cinema

10:45–1~~1:45~~ 11:55 | Student health insurance and the U.S. health care system

Luncheon | Student Center, Ballroom

12:00–1:00

Campus Tours | Tour leaders leave from the lobby of the ~~Student Center~~ Library.

~~1:30~~ 1:15 –2:30 | The last tour departs at 2:00.

Getting Around | Student Center, ~~Ballroom~~ Cinema

3:00–4:00 | Transportation system routes and ticket prices

WELCOME TO INTERNATIONAL STUDENT ORIENTATION

August 19

Dean's Welcome   Candler Chapel
9:00–9:30

Immigration Sessions   Student Center, Room 413, F-1 Visa Holders
9:30–10:30   Student Center, Room 355, J-1 Visa Holders

Refreshment Break, Commons
10:30-10:45

Health Care in the U.S.   Student Center, Cinema
10:45–11:45   Student health insurance and the U.S. health care system

Luncheon   Student Center, Ballroom
12:00–1:00

Campus Tours   Tour leaders leave from the lobby of the Student Center.
1:00–2:30   The last tour departs at 2:00.

Getting Around   Student Center, Ballroom
3:00–4:00   Transportation system routes and ticket prices

CHART/STUDENT A		
Area	**Many Other Countries**	**United States**
Formality in Class	**1.** Teachers tend to be formal.	**1.**
Frequency of Testing	**2.**	**2.** Frequent tests and quizzes.
Competition Among Students	**3.** Students tend to cooperate.	**3.**
Student Questions	**4.**	**4.** Questions are encouraged.
Age of Teachers	**5.** Older teachers are preferred.	**5.**

CHART/STUDENT B		
Area	**Many Other Countries**	**United States**
Formality in Class	**1.**	**1.** Teachers tend to be informal.
Frequency of Testing	**2.** Few tests and quizzes.	**2.**
Competition Among Students	**3.**	**3.** Students tend to compete.
Student Questions	**4.** Questions are discouraged.	**4.**
Age of Teachers	**5.**	**5.** Younger teachers are often preferred.

ROLE X

Situation 1: Police Officer Stops Driver

ROLE: Driver

You are driving along an uncongested four-lane city street. You are thinking about work or school and are not paying much attention to your driving. A police officer behind you signals you to pull over. You have no idea what your offense was. You are nervous but polite. After you learn what you did, you are very apologetic.

Situation 2: Supermarket Overcharges Customer

ROLE: Customer

You are in the checkout lane at the supermarket. The cashier is ringing up your groceries. The computer has just charged you full price for two rolls of paper towels that were on sale—two for the price of one. You are annoyed because you frequently get overcharged at this store.

Situation 3: Passenger Complains to Airline

ROLE: Passenger

You and your family have just returned to Miami from San Francisco. During the Saturday morning flight, a film that was quite violent was shown. Even though you didn't rent headphones, it was hard for you to ignore the screen. You believe that this film was a poor choice for the many children on board. You call the airline to complain.

ROLE Y

Situation 1: Police Officer Stops Driver

ROLE: Police officer

You have just stopped a driver who entered an intersection after the light turned yellow. You request the driver's license and registration. Even though the driver seems genuinely sorry and does not know it is illegal to enter an intersection on a yellow light, you give the driver a ticket anyway.

Situation 2: Supermarket Overcharges Customer

ROLE: Cashier

You rely on the computer to charge the correct prices and do not know the paper towels are on sale. You apologize for the mistake and tell the customer you will adjust the price. When you see how annoyed the customer is, you offer the paper towels free of charge.

Situation 3: Passenger Complains to Airline

ROLE: Customer service employee

Your airline selects movies that will appeal to the majority of its customers—adults traveling on business. The movie in question was rated PG-13. You ask the caller to suggest some suitable titles. You don't have time to talk with the customer and are noticeably impatient. Finally, you suggest that the caller make a formal complaint in writing.

DRIVING TEST

1. If there are no sidewalks, on which side of the street should you walk?

2. Unless otherwise posted, what is the maximum speed limit in your state?

3. If your car starts to skid on a slippery surface, should you use the brakes?

4. How should you set your car's headlights in foggy weather?

5. If you are involved in an accident with another driver, what information should you exchange?

6. If you have been drinking alcohol, what should you do before you drive?

DRIVING TEST

7. If you get drowsy while driving, what should you do?

8. If you see a flashing red light at an intersection, what should you do?

9. If you see a flashing yellow light at an intersection, what should you do?

10. If your car's brakes fail, what should you do?

11. What is the minimum speed limit on the freeways in your state?

12. If you see trouble ahead, how should you warn the driver behind you?

Strategies for Independent Learning*

In this class, most of you have become aware of how to speak more clearly. Some of you have begun to make changes in your pronunciation, both conscious and unconscious, when speaking in class. Others have begun to make changes in pronunciation outside class.

Unlearning old ways of speaking and learning new ways of speaking require continued practice in different contexts. Here are some suggestions to help you retain the progress you have made and to continue to make long-term progress on your own. Some of these suggestions are new; others are a review of Helpful Hints from the text.

Suggestion 1

✔ Reestablish your commitment to **take the time** and **make the conscious effort** to change. It won't happen automatically.

WHAT YOU CAN DO

1. Look at the pronunciation proficiency continuum in Chapter 1. Where were you at the beginning of the course? Where are you now? Where do you want to be in six months?

2. Look at the practice priorities in your "Speech Profile Summary Form" in Chapter 1 and your "Midcourse Self-Evaluation" at the end of Chapter 6. What are your current practice priorities? Write them below. Review your practice priorities every two or three weeks.

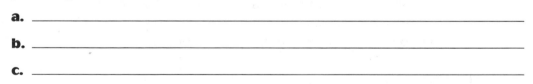

a. _____

b. _____

c. _____

Suggestion 2

✔ Try to overcome any resistance you have to sounding like a speaker of American English. Such resistance might be an obstacle to pronunciation progress.

Changing pronunciation patterns involves changes in breathing, facial expression, and sometimes even body movement. You may feel less Korean,

---

*Many principles and practice strategies included in Appendix A are based on the ideas and insights of Joan Morley and William Acton. See the *Instructor's Manual* for a list of references.

Chinese, Japanese, French, Indian, Thai, German, Greek, Italian, Arabic, Latin American, or Spanish when you speak English, but be assured that you won't lose your accent completely. You will probably always sound like a speaker of your native language.

WHAT YOU CAN DO

1. Imitate American English speakers you know and admire. Try to mimic gestures and facial expressions, as well as specific pronunciation patterns.

2. Imagine your use of American English speech patterns to be like a coat you can put on and take off at will or as the situation requires.

3. Remember that your goals are to change only those patterns that interfere with understanding and that are highly distracting to the listener.

Suggestion 3

✔ Practice regularly to achieve long-term changes in your pronunciation.

WHAT YOU CAN DO

1. Schedule a 5- to 10-minute practice session each day. Focus on your practice priorities:
   - Practice a new sound or stress pattern in words and phrases silently or in slow motion. Focus on how the pattern feels.
   - Practice a new sound or stress pattern out loud but with your eyes closed. Focus on how the pattern sounds.
   - Practice a new sound or stress pattern in sentences. Read the sentence (or thought group) and then look up and say it.
   - Practice a sound or rhythm pattern in an oral reading. Mark the reading for thought groups and for occurrences of a particular sound, stress, or rhythm pattern. Record the reading, listen to it, and evaluate it.
   - Anticipate and silently rehearse what you will say in a class, in a meeting, in a discussion, in a phone conversation, or in an oral presentation. Record it and listen to it. Monitor your pronunciation of key words related to the topic.
   - Practice in front of a mirror. Try to mimic the mouth and facial movement of speakers of American English.
   - Record yourself reading a passage of at least 300 words from your field of work or study. Listen to the recording and take notes as if in a lecture. Write the important content words and omit the less important function words. Listen again and evaluate your use of overall rhythm patterns. Did you stress the content words and reduce the function words?

2. Self-monitor your speech for a short time—five minutes—each day. Because it takes concentrated effort to be conscious of what you are saying and how you

are saying it, don't try to self-monitor much longer than five minutes each day. Choose a relaxed situation in which you have some control over the conversation.

3. Do not be anxious about errors. If you hear one, note it and go on. If it is convenient to self-correct, do so.

4. Use a technique called *tracking*. In tracking, try to repeat what a speaker of American English is saying on a word-for-word basis, following about one or two words behind the speaker. At first, follow the intonation contours, speed, stress, and rhythm patterns by humming. As you become better at tracking, add words. You can track speakers on radio and television, as well as in real situations. You can track silently or out loud.

5. Seek the support of speakers of American English. Tell trusted friends and coworkers that you have taken a course to improve your pronunciation. Tell them how they can assist you. Tell them you want to know when they don't understand you. Tell them if you want to be corrected.

6. Help speakers of American English be good informants and models. If you ask English speakers how to pronounce words, their models may be exaggerated and unnatural. Ask the informants to say words in sentences, and you will probably hear more natural pronunciations.

7. Keep an oral diary or journal. Record thoughts and events of the day on a cassette. Evaluate the recording by focusing on one pronunciation feature at a time. Listen for clear, as well as unclear, productions of particular pronunciation points.

8. Keep a list of words you encounter frequently and want to say clearly. Consult your dictionary for pronunciations. Practice the words often by saying them out loud once, then twice in a row, then three times in a row, and so on. Create typical sentences for the words or ask an English speaker to record the words in sentences for you so that you can practice by imitating the model or by speaking along with the model.

Consonants

An Overview of the Consonant Sounds of American English

The 24 Consonant Sounds

The consonant sounds of American English are represented below with phonetic symbols and key words.

Exercise 1

Repeat the sounds and key words after your teacher or the speaker on tape.

/p/ **p**ic	/f/ **f**an	/ʃ/ **sh**oe	/ŋ/ ri**ng**
/b/ **b**uy	/v/ **v**an	/ʒ/ u**s**ual	/l/ **l**ed
/t/ **t**ime	/θ/ **th**ink	/tʃ/ **ch**oose	/r/ **r**ed
/d/ **d**ime	/ð/ **th**em	/dʒ/ **j**uice	/w/ **w**e
/k/ **k**ey	/s/ **s**o	/m/ **m**y	/y/ **y**ou
/g/ **g**o	/z/ **z**oo	/n/ **n**o	/h/ **h**ow

a. Circle the consonant sounds you do *not* have in your native language.

b. Refer to your "Speech Profile Summary Form" in Chapter 1. List the consonant sounds your teacher indicated were troublesome for you.

_____   _____   _____

c. List any other consonant sounds that are difficult for you.

_____   _____   _____

Voiced and Voiceless Consonants

Consonants can be classified as voiced or voiceless. When you say a voiced consonant, the vocal cords vibrate. When you say a voiceless consonant, the vocal cords don't vibrate.

Voicing a consonant can affect word meaning. The primary difference between the consonant pairs below is whether they are voiceless or voiced.

Exercise 2

Repeat the sound/word pairs below. To monitor for voicing, place your hand on your throat or on your cheek and feel the vibration of the voiced sounds. Or cover your ears with your hands and notice that the voiced sounds are very loud, whereas the voiceless sounds are almost inaudible.

VOICELESS CONSONANTS	VOICED CONSONANTS
/p/ **p**ath	/b/ **b**ath
/t/ **t**ime	/d/ **d**ime
/k/ **c**ame	/g/ **g**ame
/f/ **f**an	/v/ **v**an
/θ/ **th**ink	/ð/ **th**em
/s/ **S**ue	/z/ **z**oo
/ʃ/ **sh**oe	/ʒ/ u**s**ual
/tʃ/ **ch**in	/dʒ/ **g**in

Except for the voiceless /h/, the remaining consonants are voiced and have no voiceless counterparts: /m/, /n/, /ŋ/, /l/, /r/, and /y/, and /w/.

Consonant Rule 1

☑ **The most important difference between voiceless and voiced consonants at the ends of words** is that the vowel sounds longer before a voiced consonant.

Exercise 3

Listen to your teacher or the speaker on tape say the word pairs below. Circle the word in each pair that seems to have a longer vowel sound. Check the "Answer Key for Appendix B."

ri**p**	ri**b**
we**d**	we**t**
ri**ch**	ri**dg**e
ba**dg**e	ba**tch**
fa**c**e	**ph**ase
le**d**	le**t**
plu**g**	plu**ck**
lea**f**	lea**v**e
hal**f**	ha**v**e

righ*t*	ri*d*e
sa*v*e	sa*f*e
play*s*	pla*c*e
sur*f*	ser*v*e

Check the answer key.

Repeat the word pairs above.

Consonant Rule 2

✓ **The most important difference between voiced and voiceless consonants at the beginnings of words** is that voiceless consonants at the beginnings of words and stressed syllables are pronounced with aspiration—the sound of escaping air.

Exercise 4

Listen to your teacher or the speaker on tape say the pairs of words below. Circle the word in each pair with the consonant that has more of a sound of escaping air.

*v*iew	*f*ew
*f*an	*v*an
*b*ore	*p*oor
a*pp*ear	a *b*eer
*p*ack	*b*ack
*g*lass	*c*lass
*c*ome	*g*um
*d*rip	*t*rip
*t*ime	*d*ime
*ch*eap	*J*eep
*ch*oke	*j*oke

Check the answer key.

Exercise 5

Put your hand, a sheet of paper, or a downy feather in front of your mouth. Say a word with a voiceless sound (e.g., *pie*). You should feel a release of air or see the paper or feather flutter.

Repeat the phrasal pairs below. Pay special attention to aspiration in the voiceless sounds.

VOICELESS (ASPIRATED)	VOICED (UNASPIRATED)
f	**v**
the last *f*ew	the last *v*iew
fix the *f*an	fix the *v*an
re*f*use the offer	re*v*iews the offer
dangerous ri*f*le	dangerous ri*v*al
p	**b**
*p*ack it up	*b*ack it up
select a *p*each	select a *b*each
*p*ouring rain	*b*oring rain
a good *p*ie	a good *b*uy
k	**g**
*c*ould swim	*g*ood swim
a full *c*lass	a full *g*lass
useless *c*lue	useless *g*lue
ba*ck*ing the purchase	ba*gg*ing the purchase

Forming Consonant Sounds

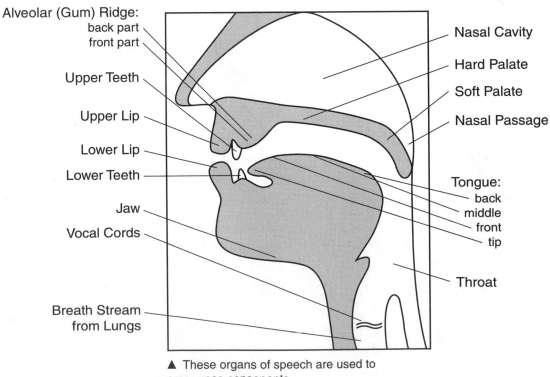

▲ These organs of speech are used to pronounce consonants.

Consonants are formed by partially or completely blocking the breath stream with the lips, tongue, gum ridge, palate (roof of the mouth), or throat. Some consonants involve completely trapping the air and then abruptly releasing it. These sounds are short and are sometimes called **stops.** Say these stops: /p/, /b/, /t/, /d/, /k/, and /g/.

Other consonants involve a partial obstruction or constriction of the breath stream. These consonants are sustainable and longer in duration. Because they can continue, they are called **continuants.** Say these continuants: /θ/, /ð/, /s/, /z/, /ʃ/, /ʒ/, /f/, and /v/.

Exercise 6

Listen to the word pairs. Notice the shorter duration of the stops and the longer duration of the continuants.

STOPS (SHORTER)	CONTINUANTS (LONGER)
lea*p*	lea*f*
wi*t*	wi*th*
fi*g*	fi*sh*
ba*ke*	bei*ge*
bea*d*	bee*f*
dea*d*	dea*th*

Two consonant sounds, /tʃ/ and /dʒ/, are called **affricates** and combine stops plus continuants. The /tʃ/ is a /t/ + /ʃ/. Say /ʃ/ . . . /ʃ/ . . . /ʃ/. Now put your tongue in position for /t/ before you release the /ʃ/ and say /tʃ/ . . . /tʃ/ . . . /tʃ/.

The /dʒ/ is a /d/ + /ʒ/. Say /ʒ/ . . . /ʒ/ . . . /ʒ/. Now put your tongue in position for /d/ before you release the /ʒ/ and say /dʒ/ . . . /dʒ/ . . . /dʒ/.

Some continuants involve directing the breath stream through the nose and are called **nasals.** Say /m/, /n/, and /ŋ/ and feel the breath stream escape through your nose. One continuant, /l/, involves directing the breath stream around the sides of the tongue and is called a **lateral.** With continuants /w/ and /y/, the organs of speech **glide** from one position to another.

The chart below shows the formation of consonant sounds. Because speaking is rapid and dynamic, however, positions for each sound will vary, depending on the speaker, the surrounding sounds, and the formality of the situation.

CONSONANT CHART

		Both Lips	Lip-Teeth	Tongue-Teeth	Tongue-Gum Ridge	Tongue-Hard Palate	Tongue-Soft Palate	Throat
Stops – Breath is stopped and released.	V–	p			t		k	
	V+	b			d		g	
Fricatives – Breath is constricted.	V–		f	θ	s	ʃ		h
	V+		v	ð	z	ʒ		
Affricates – Breath is stopped and constricted.	V–				tʃ			
	V+				dʒ			
Nasals – Breath is released through the nose.	V+	m			n		ŋ	
Liquids – Breath is not obstructed.	V+				l, r *			
Glides – Mouth glides from one position to another.	V+	w				y		

* /l/ is lateral; /r/ is retroflex

Consonant Practices

This section provides concentrated practice with the five most troublesome consonant sounds for high intermediate/advanced speakers of English. These consonant sounds are contrasted with sounds that many learners of English use as replacements.

1. Consonant 1: /θ/ as in *think*   (vs. /s/, /t/, and /f/)

2. Consonant 2: /f/ as in *fine*   (vs. /p/)

3. Consonant 3: /ʃ/ as in *she*   (vs. /tʃ/ and /s/)

4. Consonant 4: /r/ as in *right*   (vs. /l/)

5. Consonant 5: /v/ as in *vote*   (vs. /w/, /b/, and /f/)

Each consonant review includes listening activities and exercises for independent laboratory use, as well as a "Communicative Practice" section for follow-up classroom practice in pairs or small groups. If you are having difficulty with consonant sounds not included below, ask your teacher to recommend practice material from a textbook that presents a survey of all speech sounds.

Consonant 1: /θ/ as in *think* (vs. /s/, /t/, and /f/)

Fact 1. Learners of English sometimes replace the voiceless /θ/ with an /s/, /t/, or /f/ so that *thank* sounds like *sank*, *thought* sounds like *taught*, or *three* sounds like *free*. Other learners might omit the sound at the ends of words.

Fact 2. The voiceless /θ/ occurs in content words. In contrast, the voiced /ð/ occurs primarily in function words (e.g., *the, this, that*) and a few family relation words (e.g., *mother, brother*).

Listening Activity 1

Listen to the /θ/. Notice the friction-like sound of the breath stream as it passes over the tongue between the teeth.

/θ/ ... /θ/ ... /θ/ ... /θ/ ... /θ/

Listening Activity 2

Listen to the words with /θ/. Do you hear the sound at the beginning (B), in the middle (M), or at the end (E) of each word? Close your book and write B, M, or E on a piece of paper. Check the answer key.

a. think	**e.** death	**i.** south
b. three	**f.** anything	**j.** length
c. bath	**g.** Thursday	**k.** birthday
d. mathematics	**h.** thirty	**l.** month

Listening Activity 3

Listen to the word pairs. Which word of each pair has the /θ/ sound—the first or the second? Close your book and write 1 or 2 on a piece of paper. Check the answer key.

a. think	sink		**f.** path	pass
b. math	mass		**g.** sought	thought
c. truce	truth		**h.** youth	you
d. three	tree		**i.** tense	tenth
e. mat	math		**j.** thin	fin

Listening Activity 4

Listen to your teacher, the speaker on tape, or your partner say one of the prompts in each pair. Give the correct response. Check the answer key. As a pair practice, student 1 should cover responses and student 2 should cover prompts.

PROMPTS (STUDENT 1)	RESPONSES (STUDENT 2)
a. I think it's thin.	(It's not thick.)
I think it's tin.	(It's not aluminum.)
b. She took a bat.	(She wants to play baseball.)
She took a bath.	(She was dirty.)
c. It's a three.	(It's not an eight.)
It's a tree.	(It's not a bush.)
d. I think she'll be three.	(I'm almost certain she's two now.)
I think she's free.	(Her calendar looks clear.)
e. Help him. He's sinking.	(He can't swim.)
Help him. He's thinking.	(He can't solve the problem alone.)

Listening Activity 5

Listen to the paragraph. Fill in the blanks with words that have /θ/. Check the answer key.

What Makes You Thin?

What makes you _____? Most people _____ that dieting is the answer, but researchers say that exercise is the best way to be _____. In one study, _____ men who were sedentary were put on an exercise program. They walked, jogged, and ran _____ the one-year program. The first _____ the study showed was that the men who had exercised the most lost the most weight. The second _____ the study revealed was that the men who lost the most weight ate more too. The researchers _____ that fat people don't really eat a lot. Their problem is that they are inactive.

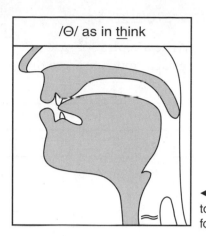

/Θ/ as in t̲h̲ink

◄ Forming the voiceless /θ/. Lightly place the tip of the tongue against the cutting edge of the upper teeth. Then force air through the contact.

Exercise 1

Repeat the words with /θ/.

think	something	with
thought	without	both
three	anything	strength
thirsty	birthday	truth
through	worthwhile	south
thank	hypothesis	north
Thursday	method	math
theory	withhold	width

Exercise 2

a. Words that contain both /θ/ and /s/, /t/, or /f/ may be especially difficult. Repeat these words.

With /s/	*With /t/*	*With /f/*
south	teeth	fourth
something	truth	fifth
synthesize	twentieth	thief
thesis	thirty	faith

b. Consonant clusters with /θ/ might also be difficult. The /θ/ is a continuant, so you need to sustain /θ/ until you say the next consonant. Repeat these words.

*thr*ee	bir*ths*
*thr*ow	mon*ths*
*thr*ough	nor*th*west

Exercise 3

Choose three words with /θ/ that you use frequently. Write a typical phrase or sentence you might say with each of the words. Practice each sentence three times.

a. _____

b. _____

c. _____

Exercise 4

Repeat the word pairs in Listening Activity 3. Make a clear distinction between /θ/ and /s/, /f/, and /t/.

Exercise 5

Practice blending the final /θ/ with the first sound in the next word. Repeat the phrases. Say each phrase as if it were one word.

fourth thing	with three colleagues
fourth sentence	with them
fourth point	with my friends
fourth house	with time
fourth time	with confidence
fourth order	with a knife

Exercise 6

Practice the boldfaced, italicized words silently. Repeat the sentences. Look up from your book as you say each sentence.

a. I'm so ***thirsty***.

b. That was ***three*** days ago.

c. The test is on ***Thursday***.

d. He grew up in the ***Southwest***.

e. Give me one ***method*** for solving the problem.

f. It's not ***worth*** your time.

g. We talked about two ***things***.

h. I'm sorry. I have ***something*** else to do right now.

Exercise 7

Record yourself reading the paragraph titled "What Makes You Thin?" in Listening Activity 5 in the answer key. Monitor the italicized words with /θ/. Then re-create the mini-lecture in your own words.

Communicative Practice

Imagine that you are a teaching assistant in an American university. You have to announce a schedule change for a design methods course. Use the information in the memo below.

   Mark and practice all words and numbers with the voiceless /θ/ before you begin. Work with a partner and take turns making the announcement.

MEMORANDUM

TO: All Design Methods 634 Teaching Assistants
RE: Schedule Change

Please make your students aware of the following changes effective September 19:

	Former Time	*New Time*
Discussion Section A	Thurs., 8:30 P.M. Classroom Bldg. Room 18	Thurs., 4:30 P.M. Classroom Bldg. Room 23
Discussion Section B	Tues., 2:00 P.M. French Bldg. Room 222	Tues., 2:30 P.M. Thurmond Hall Room 353

Consonant 2: /f/ as in *fine* (vs. /p/)

Fact 1: The /f/ sound is spelled *f (free)*, *ph (sphere)*, and *gh (tough)*.

Fact 2: Students sometimes replace the /f/ with /p/ so that *coffee* sounds like *copy*.

Listening Activity 1

Listen to /f/. Notice the friction-like sound as the breath is forced between the upper teeth and inside lower lip.

/f/ . . . /f/ . . . /f/ . . . /f/ . . . /f/

Listening Activity 2

Listen to the words with /f/. Is the /f/ at the beginning (B), in the middle (M), or at the end (E) of each word? Close your book and write B, M, or E on a piece of paper. Check the answer key.

a. find	**e.** proof	**i.** fine
b. half	**f.** reflect	**j.** belief
c. first	**g.** specific	**k.** few
d. golf	**h.** fix	**l.** yourself

Listening Activity 3

Listen to the word pairs. Does the first or second word of each pair have the /f/ sound? Close your book and write 1 or 2 on a piece of paper. Check the answer key.

a. fine	pine	**g.** pan	fan
b. coffee	copy	**h.** cheap	chief
c. paint	faint	**i.** fill	pill
d. past	fast	**j.** pool	fool
e. peel	feel	**k.** suffer	supper
f. fashion	passion	**l.** fact	pact

Listening Activity 4

Listen to your teacher, the speaker on tape, or your partner say one of the prompts in each pair. Give the correct response. Check the answer key. As a pair practice, student 1 should cover responses, and student 2 should cover prompts.

PROMPTS (STUDENT 1)	RESPONSES (STUDENT 2)
a. It's a new copy machine.	(That's why the copies are so clear.)
It's a new coffee machine.	(That's why the coffee tastes so good.)

b. It's a fact.   (Do you have proof?)

It's a pact.   (Is everyone in agreement?)

c. That's the chief executive
officer.   (That's the big boss.)

That's the cheap executive
officer.   (We never get raises.)

d. She's driving past.   (Did you see her go by?)

She's driving fast.   (She should slow down.)

e. Excuse me. Where would
I find pans?   (In the housewares department.)

Excuse me. Where would
I find fans?   (In the small appliances department.)

Listening Activity 5

Listen to the paragraph. Fill in the blanks with words that have the /f/ sound.
Check the answer key.

Videophones

In 1992, AT&T began _____ customers a video _____, a

_____ with a small color screen that allows callers to look at each other while

they are talking. _____ callers _____ to be invisible, however, a special

_____ will close the lens of the camera. Now, in addition to the popular

_____ for your cars and video _____ _____ systems that have

become almost standard in the _____ of big businesses, you can plug video

_____ into standard _____ outlets in your home.

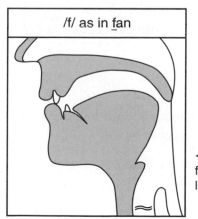

/f/ as in <u>f</u>an

◄ Forming the voiceless /f/. Gently touch the upper
front teeth to the inside lower lip. Force air through the
light contact.

Exercise 1

Repeat these words with /f/:

few	confuse	proof
function	effective	staff
first	reference	golf
feedback	different	half
fix	therefore	if
free	careful	graph
fail	office	relief
frequently	transfer	beef

Exercise 2

Words that contain both /f/ and /p/ may be difficult. Repeat these words:

friendship, follow-up, profession, payoff, playoff, proof, prefer, perfect

Consonant clusters with /f/ may also be difficult. Repeat these words.

*fl*ew	le*ft*
*fr*ee	so*ft*
*fr*om	stu*ffed*
*fl*aw	gra*phs*

Exercise 3

Choose three words with /f/ that you use frequently. Write a typical sentence you might say with each of the words. Practice saying each sentence three times.

a. _____

b. _____

c. _____

Exercise 4

Say the word pairs in Listening Activity 3. Make a clear distinction between /f/ and /p/.

Exercise 5

Practice blending the final /f/ with the first sound of the next word in the phrases below. Repeat the phrases. Say each phrase as if it were one word.

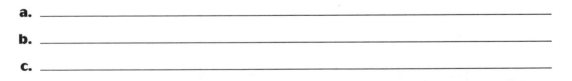

half__finished   staff__facilities

half__cooked   staff__supplies

half__done	staff__complaints
half__typed	staff__meeting
half__a cup	staff__involvement

Exercise 6

Practice the boldfaced, italicized words silently. Repeat the sentences. Look up from the book as you say the sentences.

a. I'm *fine.*

b. Which do you *prefer?*

c. What's the *first* term?

d. Did you *fill* out the *form?*

e. There are a *few* exceptions.

f. Were you *satisfied* with his explanation?

g. Have you *found* a place to live?

h. We need a new *coffee* machine for the *office.*

Exercise 7

Record yourself reading the paragraph titled "Videophones" in Listening Activity 5 in the answer key. Monitor your pronunciation of the boldfaced, italicized words with /f/. Summarize the information in your own words.

Communicative Practice

Complete these superstitions according to common beliefs in your culture. In groups of five or six, share completed sentences. Which superstitions did you have in common? Can you add one more?

Monitor your pronunciation of *if* and these words with /f/: *front, find, flies, Friday.*

1. If you spill salt, . . .

2. If a black cat crosses in front of you, . . .

3. If you find a coin, . . .

4. If you break a mirror, . . .

5. If your nose itches, . . .

6. If you blow out all of the candles on your birthday cake, . . .

7. If you tell someone your wish, . . .

8. If you begin a trip on a Friday, . . .

9. If a bird flies into your house, . . .

10. Add one of your own: _____

Consonant 3: /ʃ/ as in *she* (vs. /tʃ/ and /s/)

Fact 1: The /ʃ/ has many spellings. The most common are *sh (she)* and *-ti- (nation)*, but /ʃ/ is also spelled *-ci- (social)*, *-ssi- (mission)*, and *-ssu- (issue)*.

Fact 2: Some students replace /ʃ/ with /tʃ/ so that *share* sounds like *chair*. Other students replace /ʃ/ with /s/ so that *shine* sounds like *sign*.

Listening Activity 1

Listen to the /ʃ/ sound. Notice the easy, slow, continuous release of breath.

/ʃ/ ... /ʃ/ ... /ʃ/ ... /ʃ/ ...

Listening Activity 2

Listen to the words with /ʃ/. Do you hear the /ʃ/ at the beginning (B), in the middle (M), or at the end (E) of each word? Close your book and write B, M, or E on a piece of paper. Check the answer key.

a. share		**f.** cash	
b. sure		**g.** special	
c. rush		**h.** Spanish	
d. push		**i.** washing	
e. official		**j.** permission	

Listening Activity 3

Listen to the word pairs. Is the /ʃ/ sound in the first or the second word? Close your book and write 1 or 2 on a piece of paper. Check the answer key.

a. sheet	seat	**f.** shift	sift
b. shoe	chew	**g.** shore	chore
c. see	she	**h.** watching	washing
d. sheet	cheat	**i.** sour	shower
e. chop	shop	**j.** catch	cash

Listening Activity 4

Listen to your teacher, the speaker on tape, or your partner say one of the prompts in each pair. Give the correct response. Check the answer key. As a pair practice, student 1 should cover responses, and student 2 should cover prompts.

PROMPTS (STUDENT 1)	RESPONSES (STUDENT 2)
a. What's he washing?	(His sheets.)
What's he watching?	(A football game.)

b. It's going to shower.   (Is rain predicted?)

It's going to sour.   (Should I put it in the refrigerator?)

c. Can you catch this?   (Sure. I used to play baseball.)

Can you cash this?   (Sure. I'm going to the bank.)

d. She feels the shame.   (Even though it wasn't her fault.)

She feels the same.   (She's in complete agreement.)

Listening Activity 5

Listen to the following paragraph. Fill in the blanks with words that have the /ʃ/ sound. Check the answer key.

Shyness

About 92 million Americans are _____. Researchers are taking an interest

in _____ and have reached different conclusions. According to one study,

_____ _____ these days are more complex, and _____ is

becoming a _____ concern. Another study found that only about half of the

_____ people were tense or _____ in _____ _____, contrary

to popular belief. And still another study found that _____ people tend to be

more stable in their _____. Some psychologists think that _____ may be

inherited, whereas others think that _____ is cultural.

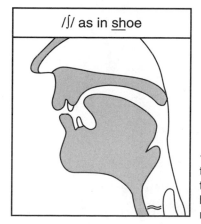

/ʃ/ as in s<u>h</u>oe

◄ Forming the voiceless /ʃ/ sound. The sides of the tongue contact the tooth ridge. Direct a rush of air along the long broad passage down the center of the tongue between the tongue and hard palate. Protrude and round the lips slightly.

Exercise 1

Repeat these words:

she	refreshing	foolish
short	machine	crash
shelf	washing	finish
shower	official	fresh
should	social	push
shoe	patient	British
shop	vacation	fish
shampoo	national	selfish

Exercise 2

Words that contain both /ʃ/ and /s/ or /tʃ/ are difficult for some students. Repeat these words:

situation, selfish, social, section, special, insurance

Verbs ending in /ʃ/ followed by the -*ing* are also sometimes difficult. Repeat these verbs until they sound natural:

cashing, wishing, pushing, punishing, washing, fishing, finishing, refreshing, rushing

Exercise 3

Choose three words with /ʃ/ that you use frequently. Write a typical phrase or sentence you might say with the words. Practice each sentence three times.

a. _____

b. _____

c. _____

Exercise 4

Repeat the word pairs in Listening Activity 3. Make a clear distinction between /ʃ/ and /s/ and between /ʃ/ and /tʃ/.

Exercise 5

Practice blending the final /ʃ/ in words with the first sound of the next word. Repeat the phrases. Say each phrase as if it were one word.

wash_sheets	finish_shopping
wash_dishes	finish_studying
wash_your hands	finish_talking
wash_the clothes	finish_eating
wash_up	finish_exercising

Exercise 6

Practice the boldfaced, italicized words silently. Repeat the sentences. Look up from your book as you say each sentence.

a. Please pass the *sugar.*

b. The tickets *should* come in the mail.

c. I'll have to *rush* to *finish* before the deadline.

d. We had time between *shifts* for a *short* lunch.

e. *She's* fluent in *English* and *Spanish.*

f. She's *anxious* to *show* you her new office.

g. Is the fish *fresh?*

h. *She's* applied for a *fellowship.*

Exercise 7

Record yourself reading the paragraph titled "Shyness" in Listening Activity 5 in the answer key. Monitor your pronunciation of the italicized words with /ʃ/. Re-create the mini-lecture in your own words.

Communicative Practice 1

In small groups of three to five students, compare and contrast the university systems in each of your countries. Monitor your pronunciation of /ʃ/ in key terms during your discussion. Share highlights of your group's discussion with the class.

USEFUL VOCABULARY WITH /ʃ/	TOPICS FOR DISCUSSION
interac**ti**on discu**ssi**on par**ti**cipa**ti**on	**a.** The interac**ti**on between the students and the professor in the classroom.
relation**sh**ip friend**sh**ip profe**ssi**onal	**b.** The relation**sh**ip between the students and the professor outside the classroom.
tui**ti**on finan**ci**al scholar**sh**ips	**c.** Costs per year. Finan**ci**al aid.
admi**ssi**on competi**ti**on pre**ssu**re	**d.** Criteria for admi**ssi**on.

Communicative Practice 2

With a small group, create nutritious breakfast, lunch, and dinner menus containing foods that have the /ʃ/ and /tʃ/ sounds (e.g., boiled **sh**rimp, macaroni and **ch**eese, **ch**ef salad).

Consonant 4: /r/ as in *right* (vs. /l/)

Fact 1: The /r/ sound is spelled *r (road)* and *wr (wrong)*.

Fact 2: Some students replace the /r/ with /l/ or /w/ so that *correct* sounds like *collect* or *rest* sounds like *west*. Other students omit the /r/ after vowels so that *heart* approximates *hot*. Finally, some students tap the tongue against the upper gum ridge to make /r/. This tongue-tap variation is not likely to cause misunderstanding.

Fact 3: Some regional dialects of American English omit the /r/ after vowels (e.g., *park, argue, fear*).

Listening Activity 1

Listen to the /r/ sound.

/r/ ... /r/ ... /r/ ... /r/ ... /r/

Listening Activity 2

Listen to the words with /r/. Do you hear the sound at the beginning (B), in the middle (M), or at the end (E) of each word? Close your book and write B, M, or E on a piece of paper. Check the answer key.

a. radio	**e.** arrive	**i.** however
b. rest	**f.** right	**j.** grew
c. here	**g.** history	**k.** brush
d. fair	**h.** around	**l.** room

Listening Activity 3

Listen to the word pairs. Which word of each pair has the /r/ sound—the first or the second? Close your book and write 1 or 2 on a piece of paper. Check the answer key.

a. crowd	cloud	**f.** run	one	**k.** rice	lice
b. wrong	long	**g.** went	rent	**l.** pot	part
c. lead	read	**h.** here	heel	**m.** lawn	learn
d. erect	elect	**i.** halt	heart	**n.** sharp	shop
e. right	light	**j.** stale	stare		

Listening Activity 4

Listen to your teacher, the speaker on tape, or your partner say one of the prompts in each pair. Give the correct response. Check the answer key. As a pair practice, student 1 should cover responses, and student 2 should cover prompts.

PROMPTS (STUDENT 1)	RESPONSES (STUDENT 2)
a. You have the long number.	(You need the short one.)
You have the wrong number.	(Hang up and dial again.)
b. Where does she pray?	(At church.)
Where does she play?	(At the playground.)
c. I watched the clouds go by.	(In the sky.)
I watched the crowds go by.	(In the street.)
d. He looks like he's bowling.	(He's holding a ball.)
He looks like he's boring.	(He has such a dull expression.)
e. Would you rake them up?	(Those leaves are killing the grass.)
Would you wake them up?	(They've been sleeping all morning.)
f. What's your favorite spot in the United States?	(I like the Southwest.)
What's your favorite sport in the United States?	(I like baseball.)

Listening Activity 5

Listen to the paragraph. Fill in the blanks with words that have the /r/ sound. Check the answer key.

Butterflies in Your Stomach

If you've ever given a _____ in front of a class or a _____ of people, you know the feeling. Your heart _____, your blood pressure _____, your hands start to shake, your throat gets _____, and you get _____ flies in your stomach. What causes your body to _____ this way? When you are nervous or _____, your glands _____ adrenaline into your bloodstream. The adrenaline causes your muscles to tense up. It also causes _____ motion in your stomach muscles. As a _____, your stomach _____ more acid than it needs for digestion. The acid feels like _____ flies in your stomach.

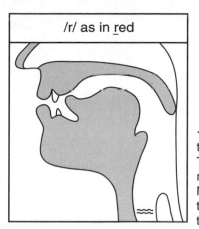

/r/ as in <u>r</u>ed

◀ Forming the voiced /r/ sound. The sides of the tongue touch the tooth ridge as if you were saying the /iʸ/ in *ear*. The tip of the tongue slightly curls back behind the gum ridge (but does not touch it). Lips are slightly rounded. Note this important distinction between /r/ and /l/: For /r/, the tip of the tongue touches nothing; for /l/, the tip of the tongue touches the gum ridge.

Exercise 1

Repeat these words with the /r/ sound:

INITIAL	BLENDS	/ɜr/ *
write	price	shirt
result	friend	burn
repeat	brown	firm
read	grow	hurt
rude	drive	hurry
routine	practice	server
robot	contract	sir
rice	free	Thursday
room	prefer	confer

*Note: When /r/ occurs after a vowel in the same syllable, sometimes the pronunciation is simply /ɜr/ as in *girl*. The /ɜr/ sound usually occurs in words spelled *-ir (bird)*, *-er (herd)*, and *-ur (turn)* and occasionally *–or (word, worry, work, and world.)*

Exercise 2

Words that contain both an /r/ and an /l/ may be especially difficult. Repeat these words:

frequently, really, rarely, clearly, early, realize, religion, learn, problem, electric, salary, large, celebrate, parallel

Exercise 3

Choose three words with /r/ that you use frequently. Write a typical phrase or sentence you might say with each of the words. Practice each sentence three times.

a. _____

b. _____

c. _____

Exercise 4

Repeat the word pairs in Listening Activity 3. Make a clear distinction between /r/ and /l/ and between /r/ and /w/.

Exercise 5

Practice the boldfaced, italicized words silently. Repeat the sentences. Look up from your book as you say each sentence.

a. Turn *right* at the next light.

b. Some bumper *stickers* say, *Arrive* alive!

c. The *calculator* is *solar powered*.

d. What's the *price* of a new set of *tires*?

e. *Marketing* meetings are held on *Fridays*.

f. They*'re* negotiating a new *trade agreement*.

g. Who's the *principal investigator* in the *research project*?

h. She was given a substantial *raise*.

i. I'll have to do one *more revision*.

Exercise 6

Record yourself reading the paragraph titled "Butterflies in Your Stomach" in Listening Activity 5 in the answer key. Monitor your pronunciation of words with /r/. Re-create the mini-lecture in your own words.

Communicative Practice

In a group of three or four students, underline and preview the pronunciation of all of the menu items with an /r/.

Student 1 plays the role of the waiter/waitress and writes down what each customer wants. Student 1 has access to descriptions of the menu items on the page following the menu. The other students are customers and order complete meals. If the customers want explanations of the entrees, they should ask the waiter.

MENU

Entrees

Served with your choice of two vegetables, a garden salad with choice of dressing, and rolls

Past Primavera	Baked Chicken Breast	Leg of Lamb
Southern Fried Chicken	Chicken Teriyaki	Fried Calamari
London Broil	Crabmeat au Gratin	Lasagna
Burritos	Sweet and Sour Shrimp	Meat Loaf

Today's Special

Broiled Flounder Fillets
Served with brown rice, fresh peas, and crusty French bread

Vegetables	*Beverages*
French-fried potatoes	Fresh brewed coffee
Sliced tomatoes with basil	Tea—hot or iced
Broccoli spears	Soft drinks
Zucchini-carrot medley	Milk
Corn on the cob	Lemonade
French-style green beans	
Stir fry veggies	

Desserts

Fresh fruit sorbet—assorted flavors	Fresh strawberries—in season
Blueberry pie a la mode	Hot fudge ice-cream sundae
Carrot cake	

Menu adapted from "Eating Better When Eating Out," U.S. Department of Agriculture, Home and Garden Bulletin No. 232-11.

INFORMATION FOR STUDENT 1 (WAITER)

Pasta Primavera
Ribbons of fettuccini and
fresh vegetables tossed
in a yogurt sauce,
sprinkled with Parmesan
cheese

Baked Chicken Breast
Boneless breast of
chicken baked in a delicate
lemon-basil sauce

Leg of Lamb
Marinated in red wine and
rosemary

Southern Fried Chicken
Fried to a crispy golden
brown

Chicken Teriyaki
Grilled strips of chicken
marinated in spicy
teriyaki sauce

Fried Calamari
Fried in a light batter

London Broil
Grilled strips of flank
steak served with fresh
mushrooms; cooked
to order

Crabmeat au Gratin
Crabmeat in a creamy
cheese sauce, baked to
a delicate brown

Lasagna
Made with Italian sausage
and fresh pasta

Burritos
Your choice of beef,
chicken, or beans; served
with rice and fresh salsa

Sweet and Sour Shrimp
Batter-fried shrimp
covered with a tangy
sweet and sour sauce

Meat Loaf
Low-fat version made with
lean ground beef

Choice of Salad Dressings:
House Dressing—Vinaigrette
Ranch
Blue Cheese
French
Thousand Island

BEYOND THE PRONUNCIATION CLASS: GOING TO LUNCH

Bring menus from nearby restaurants to class. Compare dishes and prices.
Practice ordering dishes with /r/ and /l/. Make plans to go to lunch together.

Consonant 5: /v/ as in *vote* (vs. /w/, /b/, and /f/)

Fact 1: Some students replace the /v/ with a /w/ and vice versa so that *veal* sounds like *wheel* and *while* sounds like *vile*. Other students replace the /v/ with a /b/ so that *very* sounds like *berry*. Still other students replace the final voiced /v/ with the voiceless /f/ so that *have* sounds like *half*.

Listening Activity 1

Listen to the /v/ sound.

/v/ ... /v/ ... /v/ ... /v/ ... /v/

Listening Activity 2

Listen to the words with /v/. Do you hear the /v/ sound at the beginning (B), in the middle (M), or at the end (E) of each word? Close your book and write B, M, or E on a piece of paper. Check the answer key.

a. visit	**f.** heavy
b. video	**g.** novel
c. develop	**h.** value
d. twelve	**i.** save
e. vote	**j.** level

Listening Activity 3

Listen to the word pairs. Which word of each pair has the /v/ sound—the first or the second? Close your book and write 1 or 2 on a piece of paper. Check the answer key.

a. very	wary	**h.** very	berry
b. vie	why	**i.** volt	bolt
c. west	vest	**j.** boats	votes
d. veil	whale	**k.** ban	van
e. wheel	veal	**l.** leaf	leave
f. verse	worse	**m.** have	half
g. evoke	awoke	**n.** lover	lower

Listening Activity 4

Listen to your teacher, the speaker on tape, or your partner say one of the prompts in each pair. Give the correct response. Check the answer key. As a pair practice, student 1 should cover responses, and student 2 should cover prompts.

PROMPTS (STUDENT 1)	RESPONSES (STUDENT 2)
a. Where did you put the veal?	(In the freezer.)
Where did you put the wheel?	(On the bike.)
b. What kind of wine did you get?	(A dry red wine.)
What kind of vine did you get?	(One with blue flowers.)
c. They evoke her.	(They remind me of her.)
They awoke her.	(They didn't want her to oversleep.)
d. What happened with the vote?	(Our candidate won.)
What happened with the boat?	(The engine died.)
e. He's serving in Hawaii.	(He's been in the navy for two years.)
He's surfing in Hawaii.	(He loves to ride the waves.)

Listening Activity 5

Listen to the paragraph. Fill in the blanks with words that have the /v/ sound. Check the answer key.

Valentine's Day*

For _____ 100 years, it has been popular to _____ cards, flowers, gifts, and other tokens of _____ on February 14, St. Valentine's Day in the United States. There are _____ explanations for the origin of this holiday; _____, the most believable is that St. _____ Day is a _____ of a February 15th Roman festival. During this _____, bachelors picked names of women to _____ who their "valentine" or _____ would be for the coming year. The couples then exchanged gifts and sometimes _____ became engaged.

*Source: *World Book Encyclopedia*, Chicago: World Book, Inc., Vol. 20, 1992, p. 277.

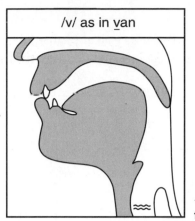

/v/ as in v̲an

◄ Forming the voiced /v/ sound. Lightly touch the upper teeth to the inside of the lower lip. Voice the sound.

Exercise 1

Repeat these words with /v/:

video	never	leave
valid	invest	save
victim	divide	above
vice president	develop	alive
velocity	seven	improve
vacation	movie	arrive
vegetables	advice	active
visit	heavy	you've

Exercise 2

Words with /v/ and /w/, /b/, or /f/ may be especially difficult. Repeat these words:

With /w/	With /b/	With /f/
vowel	behavior	forgive
wives	vibration	favor
we've	believe	fever

Exercise 3

Choose three words with /v/ that you use frequently. Write a typical phrase or sentence you might say with each of the words. Practice each sentence three times.

a. _____

b. _____

c. _____

Exercise 4

Repeat the word pairs in Listening Activity 3. Make a clear distinction between /v/ and /w/, /v/, /b/, and /f/.

Exercise 5

Practice blending the final /v/ with the first sound of the next word in the phrases below. Repeat the phrases. Say each phrase as if it were one word.

leave valuables	save victims
leave friends	save books
leave home	save text
leave together	save money
leave alone	save information

Exercise 6

Practice the boldfaced, italicized words silently. Repeat the sentences. Look up from the book as you say each sentence.

a. Would you do me a *favor?*

b. Where did you go on your *vacation?*

c. Which *movie* did you see?

d. What kind of *advice* did she *give* you?

e. Should I *save* it or *invest* it?

f. After *twelve* years of marriage, they got a *divorce.*

g. I'd like to *invite* you to my *anniversary* party.

h. When can we *leave?*

i. His *fever* got worse and worse.

Now circle the words above that begin with a /w/ sound. Say the sentences again and focus on pronouncing the /w/.

Exercise 7

Record yourself reading the paragraph titled "Valentine's Day" in Listening Activity 5 in the answer key. Monitor the italicized words with /v/. Re-create the mini-lecture in your own words.

Communicative Practice

In a group of three to five students, discuss vacation time in your countries. Monitor for the /v/ sound in the key vocabulary listed below. Be careful to use /w/, not /v/, in these words: *worker*, *white-collar*, *one*, and *week*. Report the highlights of your group's discussion to the class.

USEFUL VOCABULARY WITH /v/	TOPICS FOR DISCUSSION
*v*ary ha*v*e a*v*erage	**a.** How long is the a*v*erage *v*acation for blue-collar workers in your country?
se*v*en e*v*ery *v*acation fi*v*e	**b.** How long is the a*v*erage *v*acation for white-collar workers in your country?
ser*v*ice deser*v*e	**c.** What is the relationship between length of ser*v*ice in a company and length of *v*acation?
go*v*ernment	**d.** Do workers in your country usually take all of the *v*acation they deser*v*e? Do any laws in your country relate to *v*acation time?
tra*v*el *v*isit o*v*erseas dri*v*e	**e.** How do people in your country like to spend their *v*acations?

PRIME-TIME PRACTICE

Investigate local volunteer opportunities in the newspaper. Report back to the class.

Appendix

Vowels

An Overview of the Vowel Sounds of American English

The vowel sounds of American English are classified as front or back and high or low. This warm-up exercise introduces vowel classification.

Exercise 1

1. Put your finger on your upper lip. Compare /iʸ/ as in *me* with /uʷ/ as in *you*: What happens?

   With front vowels like /iʸ/, the lips are _____.

   With back vowels like /uʷ/, the lips are _____.

2. Put you finger on your chin. Compare /iʸ/ as in *me* with /ɑ/ as in *f**a**ther*. What happens?

   With high vowels like /iʸ/, the jaw (and tongue) are _____.

   With low vowels like /ɑ/, the jaw (and tongue) are _____.

Front Vowels

☑ Front vowels are made with the *front* of the tongue arched. Beginning with the first front vowel /iʸ/, the front part of the tongue is high in the mouth. The tongue and jaw drop lower and lower as you move down the list of front vowels. Front vowels are also made with the lips spread in varying degrees.

Exercise 2

Repeat the sounds and the key words after your teacher or the speaker on tape:

Vowel 1. /iʸ/   h**e**, s**ee**, f**ee**t, m**ea**t

Vowel 2. /ɪ/   h**i**t, **i**f, p**i**ck

Vowel 3. /eʸ/   m**ay**, **A**sia, f**a**ce, p**ai**n

Vowel 4. /ɛ/   m**e**t, l**e**t, d**ea**d

Vowel 5. /æ/   m**a**d, **a**sk, c**a**sh

/iʸ/ /ɪ/ /eʸ/ /ɛ/ /æ/

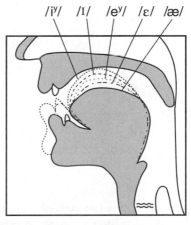

▲ The tongue position for front vowels

Central Vowels

☑ Central vowels are made with the *middle* of the tongue slightly arched. The tongue and jaw are higher for /ʌ/ and /ə/ than for /ɑ/. The lips are neither spread nor rounded for central vowels.

Exercise 3

Repeat the sounds and key words after your teacher or the speaker on tape.

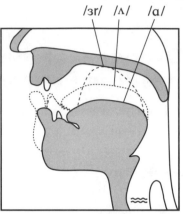

Vowel 6.   /ɜr/   g*ir*l, h*er*, t*ur*n

Vowel 7.*   /ʌ/   n*u*t, *u*p, d*u*mb

            /ə/   *a*bout, c*o*ncern

Vowel 8.   /ɑ/   n*o*t, b*o*ss, c*o*ncert, f*a*ther

▲ The tongue position for central vowels

Back Vowels

☑ Back vowels are made with the *back* part of the tongue arched. Beginning with the first back vowel /uʷ/, the back part of the tongue is high. The tongue and jaw drop lower and lower as you move down the list of back vowels. Back vowels are also made with the lips rounded in varying degrees.

Exercise 4

Repeat the sounds and the key words after your teacher or the speaker on tape.

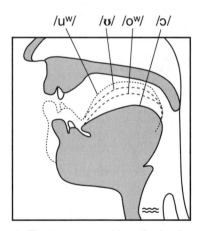

Vowel 9.   /uʷ/   t*oo*, f*oo*d, r*u*de, fl*ew*, j*ui*ce

Vowel 10.   /ʊ/   t*oo*k, f*oo*t, sh*oul*d, p*u*t

Vowel 11.   /oʷ/   n*o*, l*ow*, h*o*pe, l*oa*n

Vowel 12.   /ɔ/   l*aw*, c*au*se, b*o*rn

Note: Some speakers of American English do not distinguish between vowel 8, /ɑ/ as in c*o*t, and vowel 12, /ɔ/ as in c*au*ght.

▲ The tongue positions for back vowels

Diphthongs

☑ Diphthongs are combinations of two vowel sounds. Your mouth moves and changes shape as you pronounce diphthongs.

---

*Vowel 7 has two symbols. We use the first /ʌ/ in **stressed** words and syllables like c*u*t and *u*nder and the second /ə/ in **unstressed** words and syllables like w*a*s and *a*lone.

Exercise 5

Repeat the three diphthongs and the key words after your teacher or the speaker on tape.

Vowel 13. /aɪ/   t*ie*, l*i*k*e*, b*y*

Vowel 14. /aʊ/   *ou*t, l*ou*d, n*ow*

Vowel 15. /ɔɪ/   t*oy*, v*oi*ce

Vowel Chart

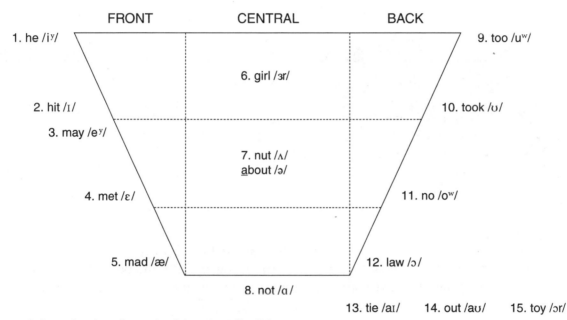

▲ The vowel chart showing all vowels of American English

1. Look at the vowel chart and circle the sounds that are completely different from those in your native language.

2. Refer to your "Speech Profile Summary Form" in Chapter 1. Which vowel sounds did your teacher indicate were troublesome for you?

_____   _____   _____

3. Are any other vowel sounds difficult for you? List them below.

_____   _____   _____

Tense and Lax Vowels

☑ The vowels /iʸ/ *(he)*, /eʸ/ *(made)*, /uʷ/ *(too)*, and /oʷ/ *(no)* are pronounced with muscle tension. They are longer in duration. The remaining vowels are shorter in duration and are made with the muscles in a more relaxed (lax) position.

Exercise 6

Many students have trouble hearing and pronouncing the difference between the pairs below. Repeat the sound/word pairs. Notice your face, lip, and tongue muscles tense and relax.

TENSE	LAX
/iʸ/ he	/ɪ/ hit
/eʸ/ made	/ɛ/ met
/uʷ/ too	/ʊ/ took
/oʷ/ no	/ɔ/ law

A HELPFUL HINT

If you have trouble hearing the difference between two vowel sounds, ask a native speaker to whisper the vowels. You may be able to perceive the difference in quality more easily.

Exercise 7

Listen as your teacher whispers the sound pairs below. Can you hear the difference? Now watch as your teacher mimes the sound pairs below. Notice the mouth movement toward a second sound in the tense vowels. Notice the static position for the lax vowels.

TENSE	LAX
/iʸ/ he	/ɪ/ hit
/eʸ/ made	/ɛ/ met
/uʷ/ too	/ʊ/ took
/oʷ/ no	/ɔ/ law

Note: Tense vowels are represented with a second smaller symbol because they are not pure. They move from one vowel sound toward a second vowel sound. To pronounce these vowels correctly, your mouth has to move and change shape.

Vowel Practices

This section provides concentrated practice with vowel sounds that are especially troublesome for intermediate to advanced speakers of English. Five vowel sounds are reviewed and contrasted with sounds many learners of English use as replacements:

1. Vowel 2: /ɪ/ as in *hit*   (vs. Vowel 1: /iʸ/ as in *he*)
2. Vowel 4: /ɛ/ as in *met*   (vs. Vowel 3: /eʸ/ as in *made*; Vowel 5: /æ/ as in *mad*)
3. Vowel 7: /ʌ/ as in *nut*   (vs. Vowel 8: /ɑ/ as in *not*)
4. Vowel 10: /ʊ/ as in *took*   (vs. Vowel 9: /uʷ/ as in *too*)
5. Vowel 8: /ɑ/ as in *not*   (vs. Vowel 11: /oʷ/ as in *no*)

Each vowel review includes listening activities and exercises for independent laboratory use, as well as a "Communicative Practice" section for follow-up classroom pair practice. The "Answer Key for Appendix C" is at the end of the text.

You will notice that vowel spellings are more varied and less predictable than consonant spellings. You may also notice that it is harder to see and feel the tongue position for vowels. As a result, you need to rely more on listening to judge accuracy.

If you have difficulty with vowel sounds not included here, ask your teacher to recommend a textbook that surveys all speech sounds.

1. Vowel 2: /ɪ/ as in *hit* (vs. Vowel 1: /iʸ/ as in *he*)

Fact 1: The /ɪ/ is a pure vowel; it is short in duration. The /ɪ/ is longer in duration and glides upward toward the /y/ sound.

Fact 2: Many students confuse /iʸ/ and /ɪ/ so that *fit* sounds like *feet* and *eat* sounds like *it*.

Listening Activity 1

Listen to /ɪ/.

> /ɪ/ . . . /ɪ/ . . . /ɪ/ . . . /ɪ/

Now listen to /ɪ/ contrasted with /iʸ/.

> /ɪ/ . . . /iʸ/ . . . /ɪ/ . . . /iʸ/ . . ./ɪ/ . . . /iʸ/

Listening Activity 2

Listen to the words with /ɪ/.

> hit, disk, did, give, with, miss, inch, wish, city, minute, live, consider, visit

Listening Activity 3

Listen to the word pairs. Which word in each pair has the /ɪ/ sound—the first or the second? Close your book and write 1 or 2 on a separate piece of paper. Check the answer key.

a. hit	heat	**f.** live	leave
b. it	eat	**g.** seen	sin
c. heel	hill	**h.** list	least
d. deed	did	**i.** will	wheel
e. feet	fit	**j.** sleep	slip

Listening Activity 4

Listen to your teacher, the speaker on tape, or your partner say one of the prompts in each pair. Give the correct response. Check the answer key. As a pair practice, student 1 should cover responses, and student 2 should cover prompts.

PROMPTS (STUDENT 1)	RESPONSES (STUDENT 2)
a. Did you slip?	(Yes, on the ice.)
Did you sleep?	(Yes, for 10 hours.)
b. Those were beautiful pitches.	(It was a great baseball game.)
Those were beautiful peaches.	(It was a good crop.)
c. Is the patient going to live?	(Yes. Her injuries weren't serious.)
Is the patient going to leave?	(Yes. She's packing her bags now.)

d. Did you hit it?   (Yes, with the hammer.)

Did you heat it?   (Yes, in the microwave.)

e. Where should I put the pills?   (In the medicine chest.)

Where should I put the peels?   (In the garbage.)

Listening Activity 5

Listen to the following paragraph. Fill in the blanks with the words that have the /ɪ/ sound in stressed words and syllables. Check the answer key.

Drinking and Health Risks*

People often _____ a glass to toast good health. _____ may indeed lower the _____ of several diseases, according to some interesting _____ released by the Harvard School of Public Health. Researchers found that up to one to two _____ each day diminished the _____ of heart attack, stroke, and fatal heart disease by about twenty-_____ percent in men and up to _____ percent in _____. One researcher warned, however, that women with a family _____ of breast cancer should _____ drinking because alcohol is _____ to a higher risk of breast cancer.

*Source: Beth Weinhouse, "Your Health," *Redbook*, January 1992, p. 19.

Exercise 1

Repeat the words with /ɪ/.

*i*f	h*i*t
*i*ll	f*i*t
*i*nto	l*i*ve
*i*ncrease, n.	s*i*t
*i*mage	l*i*st
*i*ncidence	w*i*n
*i*nnocent	cons*i*der
*i*nterstate	b*u*siness

Exercise 2

Choose three words with /ɪ/ that you use frequently. Write typical sentences you might say with the words. Practice each sentence three times.

a. _____

b. _____

c. _____

Exercise 3

Repeat the word pairs in Listening Activity 3. Make a clear distinction between /ɪ/ and /iʸ/.

Exercise 4

Practice the boldfaced, italicized words silently. Repeat the sentences. Look up from your book as you say each sentence.

a. Dollar **bills** usually wear out in less than two years.

b. My dentist found **six** cavities.

c. He's five feet nine **inches** tall.

d. Put the **fish** and **chicken** in the freezer.

e. What's your favorite **city** to visit?

f. I **live** in the **fifth** house on the right.

g. Did she **fix** the **printer?**

h. What's your **opinion?**

Exercise 5

Record yourself reading the paragraph titled "Drinking and Health Risks" in Listening Activity 5 in the answer key. Monitor your pronunciation of the italicized words with /ɪ/. Summarize the passage in your own words.

Communicative Practice

Practice the /ɪ/ sound as you create a "wish list." Pick the five items that in your opinion would most improve the quality of life. Number the five items in order of importance. Feel free to add items to the list.

In small groups of four to six students, discuss the items most important to you and justify your choices. Try to reach consensus with your group on the top two items.

Mark words with /ɪ/ in the list below. Practice them. Practice words with /ɪ/ that are likely to occur during the discussion: *if, think, wish, opinion, pick, list, important, individual, improve,* and *fifth.*

WISH LIST

INDIVIDUAL	GROUP	
_____	_____	Quality education for everyone
_____	_____	More free time
_____	_____	Drug-free world
_____	_____	Human colonies in space
_____	_____	Personal robots
_____	_____	End to prejudice
_____	_____	Housing for the homeless
_____	_____	Cures for deadly diseases
_____	_____	Adequate health care for everyone
_____	_____	Crime-free cities
_____	_____	More time with family
_____	_____	World peace
_____	_____	Full employment
_____	_____	End to hunger
_____	_____	Nonpolluting energy sources

2. Vowel 4: /ɛ/ as in *met* (vs. Vowel 3: /eʸ/ as in *made*; Vowel 5: /æ/ as in *mad*)

Fact 1. The /ɛ/ and /æ/ are pure vowels; they are short in duration. The /eʸ/ is longer in duration and glides upward toward a /y/ sound.

Fact 2. Many students replace the /ɛ/ with /eʸ/ and vice versa so that *let* sounds like *late* and *paper* sounds like *pepper.* Other students may use an approximation of the /ɛ/ for the /æ/ sound so that *bad* sounds like *bed.*

Listening Activity 1

Listen to /ɛ/.

/ɛ/ . . . /ɛ/ . . . /ɛ/ . . . /ɛ/ . . . /ɛ/

Now listen to the contrast between /ɛ/ and /eʸ/.

/ɛ/ . . . /eʸ/ . . . /ɛ/ . . . /eʸ/ . . . /ɛ/ . . . /eʸ/

Listening Activity 2

Listen to the words with /ɛ/.

let, yes, end, dead, met, left, guess, better, never, chemistry, effective

Listening Activity 3

Listen to the word pairs. Does the first or the second word in each pair have the /ɛ/ sound? Close your book and write 1 or 2 on a separate piece of paper. Check the answer key.

a. late	let	**e.** taste	test	**i.** guess	gas
b. date	debt	**f.** men	main	**j.** men	man
c. edge	age	**g.** fell	fail	**k.** taxes	Texas
d. wet	wait	**h.** later	letter	**l.** celery	salary

Listening Activity 4

Listen to your teacher, the speaker on tape, or your partner say one of the prompts in each pair. Give the correct response. Check the answer key. As a pair practice, student 1 should cover responses, and student 2 should cover prompts.

PROMPTS (STUDENT 1)	RESPONSES (STUDENT 2)
a. Could you buy some black pepper for me?	(For dinner tonight.)
Could you buy some black paper for me?	(For my art project.)
b. He just left.	(I'm sorry you missed him.)
He just laughed.	(He thought it was funny.)

c. How did you like the test? (It was hard.)

How did you like the taste? (It was too spicy.)

d. I met the men you work with. (Did you like them?)

I met the man you work with. (Did you like him?)

e. It's the right edge. (Nice and sharp.)

It's the right age. (Not too old and not too young.)

Listening Activity 5

Listen to the following paragraph. Fill in the blanks with words that have the /ɛ/ sound in stressed words and syllables. Check the answer key.

Airbags

The airbag has become standard equipment in every new car. It is stored in the

_____ of the steering wheel and, in an accident, quickly inflates to _____

save a driver's life. But how does it work? The airbag has electronic _____ that

can feel a crash as it begins to happen. The sensors _____ off a small can of

nitrogen gas, which rushes into the bag. The soft bag _____ the driver and

_____ it deflates. Airbags are only useful in _____ -on or rear- _____

accidents. During a side collision, a driver needs a seat _____ for protection.

Exercise 1

Repeat the words with /ɛ/.

edge	**e**ditor	m**e**t	n**e**ver
any	**e**ffort	b**e**tter	g**ue**ss
end	**e**xam	l**e**t	s**e**ll
exit	**e**nter	t**e**st	s**e**nd

Exercise 2

Choose three words with /ɛ/ that you use frequently. Write typical sentences you might say with the words. Practice each sentence three times.

a. _____

b. _____

c. _____

Exercise 3

Repeat the word pairs in Listening Activity 3. Make a clear distinction between /ɛ/ and /eʸ/ and between /ɛ/ and /æ/.

Exercise 4

Practice the boldfaced, italicized words silently. Notice that the /ɛ/ occurs in the stressed syllables of these words. Repeat the sentences. Look up from your book as you say the sentences.

   a. My *relatives left yesterday.*

   b. That was an *excellent question.*

   c. Did you *forget* to *send* the *letter?*

   d. The *presidential election* is *next November.*

   e. My *best friend sent* me this *present.*

   f. I've *already spent everything* that you *lent* to me.

   g. Take the *elevator* to the *second* floor.

   h. The *recipe* calls for a teaspoon of black *pepper.*

Exercise 5

Record yourself reading the paragraph titled "Airbags" in Listening Activity 5 in the answer key. Monitor your pronunciation of the italicized words with /ɛ/. Summarize the passage in your own words.

Communicative Practice

Work in pairs to create a graph depicting temperatures around the world. Student 1 has the incomplete temperature chart on page 201. Student 2 has the incomplete chart on page 202. Without looking at your partner's chart, obtain the missing information from your partner.

   Practice and monitor words with /ɛ/ that are likely to occur: *November, weather, temperature, seventy, seven, Mexico,* and *twenty.* Be sure to use the /eʸ/, not /ɛ/, in these words: *range, eight,* and *eighty.*

WORLD WEATHER FOR NOVEMBER* (Student 1)

City	Temperature Range in Fahrenheit Degrees
_____	53–66
Beijing	28–48
Budapest	33–47
Cairo	57–__
_____	53–84
Hong Kong	65–74
_____	46–__
Miami	66–__
Moscow	26–35
San Juan	__–__
Tokyo	43–60

WORLD WEATHER FOR NOVEMBER* (Student 2)

City	Temperature Range in Fahrenheit Degrees
Athens	53–66
Beijing	__–48
_____	33–__
Cairo	__–77
Delhi	53–84
Hong Kong	__–__
Mexico City	46–67
_____	66–77
Moscow	__–35
_____	77–84
Tokyo	43–60

With your partner, create a graph that clearly shows the temperature differences among the cities listed. Where would you most like to visit and least like to visit during the month of November?

*Source: Conway, McKinley, and Linda L. Liston (eds.). *The Weather Handbook,* Atlanta: Conway Data, Inc., 1999.

3. Vowel 7: /ʌ/ as in *nut* (vs. Vowel 8: /ɑ/ as in *not*)

Fact 1. The /ʌ/ is a central vowel. It is neutral because the tongue and jaw are relaxed and the lips are neither rounded nor spread.

Fact 2. Many students replace /ʌ/ with /ɑ/ and vice versa so that *luck* sounds like *lock* and *shot* sounds like *shut*.

Listening Activity 1

Listen to the /ʌ/ sound.

/ʌ/ ... /ʌ/ ... /ʌ/ ... /ʌ/ ... /ʌ/

Listen to /ʌ/ contrasted with /ɑ/.

/ʌ/ ... /ɑ/ ... /ʌ/ ... /ɑ/ ... /ʌ/ ... /ɑ/

Listening Activity 2

Listen to the words with /ʌ/.

*u*p, b*u*t, f*u*n, c*u*t, l*u*ck, *u*nder, *u*gly, s*u*pper, st*u*dy, p*u*blic, l*o*ve, c*o*me, m*o*ney

Listening Activity 3

Listen to the word pairs. Does the first or the second word in each pair have the /ʌ/ sound? Close your book and write 1 or 2 on a separate piece of paper. Check the answer key.

a. bomb	bum	**f.** box	bucks
b. robber	rubber	**g.** color	collar
c. come	calm	**h.** duck	dock
d. fund	fond	**i.** boss	bus
e. shut	shot	**j.** stuck	stock

Listening Activity 4

Listen to your teacher, the speaker on tape, or your partner say one of the prompts in each pair. Give the correct response. Check the answer key. As a pair practice, student 1 should cover responses, and student 2 should cover prompts.

PROMPTS (STUDENT 1)	RESPONSES (STUDENT 2)
a. Is that a duck?	(Yes. It has feathers.)
Is that a dog?	(Yes. It has fur.)
b. I need a cup.	(For coffee.)
I need a cop.	(For protection.)

c. What an ugly collar.   (I hate buttons on collars.)

What an ugly color.   (I hate that shade of green.)

d. This is a hard nut.   (I can't crack it.)

This is a hard knot.   (I can't untie it.)

e. Was your luck good?   (No. I lost.)

Was your lock good?   (No. It broke.)

Listening Activity 5

Listen to the following paragraph. Fill in the blanks with words that have the /ʌ/ sound in stressed words and syllables. Check the answer key.

Foreign-Born Numbers Are Up*

In a 1997 _____ , the Census Bureau reports that nearly _____ in 10 residents of the United States was foreign born. The number is nearly _____ the percentage of foreign born in 1970 (4.8%). _____ of the foreign-born population—one third of all immigrants—resides in California. New York ranks second and Florida third. The _____ study also includes where immigrants are _____ . One of every two foreign–born residents _____ from Central and South America and the Caribbean.

*Source: U.S. Census Bureau, "Foreign Born Population in the U.S.: March 1997 (Update)."

Exercise 1

Repeat the words with /ʌ/.

up	b**u**s
under	j**u**st
ugly	s**u**n
umpire	l**u**nch
uncle	l**u**ck
ulcer	m**o**ney
ultimate	s**o**mebody
upkeep	c**o**lor

Exercise 2

Choose three words with /ʌ/ that you use frequently. Write typical sentences you might say with the words. Practice each sentence three times.

a. _____

b. _____

c. _____

Exercise 3

Repeat the word pairs in Listening Activity 3. Make a clear distinction between /ʌ/ and /ɑ/.

Exercise 4

Practice the boldfaced, italicized words silently. Repeat the sentences. Look up from your book as you say each sentence.

a. Let's *discuss* your *assumptions*.

b. Do you have *enough money* for *lunch?*

c. Are you going to *study* during *summer* quarter?

d. We have *another* meeting on *Monday?*

e. I *wonder* what we're having for *supper*.

f. The *customer* ordered a *dozen* roses.

g. He presented his *results* in his *introduction*.

h. *x* is a *function* of *y*.

Exercise 5

Record yourself reading the paragraph titled "Foreign-Born Numbers Are Up," in Listening Activity 5 in the answer key. Monitor your pronunciation of the italicized words with /ʌ/.

Communicative Practice

Whom do you trust? Each year the Gallup poll asks Americans to rank professions for "honesty and ethical standards." How would you rank these professions?

Write the professions in order from most to least trusted. Compare your rankings with those of your partner. Don't forget to use /ʌ/ each time you use the word *trust*. Check the answer key to learn how your responses compared with Gallup's 1998 list.

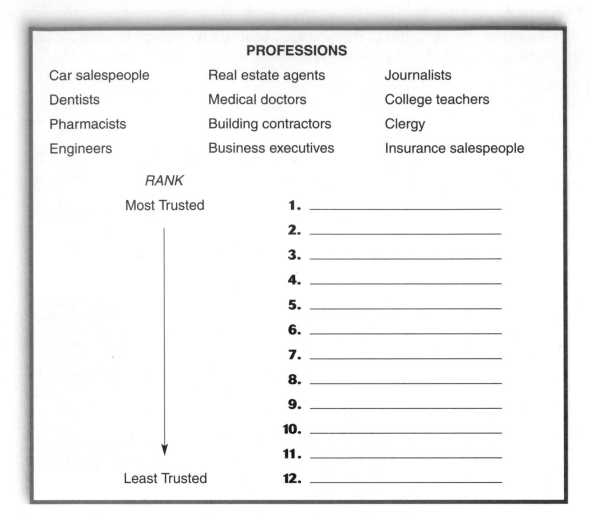

PROFESSIONS

Car salespeople	Real estate agents	Journalists
Dentists	Medical doctors	College teachers
Pharmacists	Building contractors	Clergy
Engineers	Business executives	Insurance salespeople

RANK

Most Trusted

1. _____

2. _____

3. _____

4. _____

5. _____

6. _____

7. _____

8. _____

9. _____

10. _____

11. _____

Least Trusted   12. _____

4. Vowel 10: /ʊ/ as in *took* (vs. Vowel 9: /uʷ/ as in *too*)

Fact 1. The /ʊ/ is a pure vowel and is short in duration. The /uʷ/ is longer in duration and glides toward a /w/ sound.

Fact 2. Many students confuse /ʊ/ for /uʷ/ so that *pull* sounds like *pool* and *fool* sounds like *full*. Some students also replace the /ʊ/ with /ʌ/ so that *look* sounds like *luck*.

Listening Activity 1

Listen to /ʊ/.

/ʊ/ . . . /ʊ/ . . . /ʊ/ . . . /ʊ/ . . . /ʊ/

Now listen to /ʊ/ contrasted with /uʷ/.

/ʊ/ . . . /uʷ/ . . . /ʊ/ . . . /uʷ/ . . . /ʊ/ . . . /uʷ/

Listening Activity 2

Listen to these words with /ʊ/:

look, took, cook, foot, good, put, full, should, wouldn't, bookcase, understood

Listening Activity 3

Listen to the word pairs. Does the first or second word in each pair have the /ʊ/ sound? Close your book and write 1 or 2 on a separate piece of paper. Check the answer key.

a. should	shooed		**e.** who'd	hood
b. pool	pull		**f.** look	luck
c. fool	full		**g.** took	tuck
d. stood	stewed		**h.** cud	could

Listening Activity 4

Listen to your teacher, the speaker on tape, or your partner say one of the prompts in each pair. Give the correct response. Check the answer key. As a pair practice, student 1 should cover responses, and student 2 should cover prompts.

PROMPTS (STUDENT 1)	RESPONSES (STUDENT 2)
a. Can you clean this black soot right away?	(It's all over the fireplace.)
Can you clean this black suit right away?	(I need to wear it this afternoon.)
b. He has no more pull.	(He's lost all of his influence.)
He has no more pool.	(He'll have to swim someplace else.)

c. We can't eat until the meat
has stood for an hour.   (It needs to cool.)

We can't eat until the meat
has stewed for an hour.   (It needs to be tender.)

d. They took their shirts in.   (To the cleaners.)

They tuck their shirts in.   (To their pants.)

Listening Activity 5

Listen to the following paragraph. Fill in the blanks with words that have the /ʊ/ sound in stressed words or syllables. Check the answer key.

Eating Out

People in the United States are spending less time _____ and more time eating out in restaurants. In fact, many people in the United States eat out on the average of four times a week. If you invite someone to join you for dinner in a restaurant, here are some general guidelines. You _____ phone first to find out whether you need a reservation. When you invite someone out to dinner, you _____ be prepared to pay the bill. However, sometimes the guests _____ rather pay so that they won't feel indebted to you. When the bill arrives, _____ to see whether the tip has been added to the cost of the food. Most restaurants do not add the tip to the bill. You _____ leave a tip equal to 15 percent of the bill if the service was adequate. If the restaurant is expensive or if the service was especially _____, you _____ leave up to 20 percent of the bill.

Exercise 1

Repeat the words with /ʊ/.

p**u**sh	underst**oo**d
p**u**ll	g**oo**d-bye
f**u**ll	w**ou**ld
t**oo**k	c**ou**ld
c**oo**k	sh**ou**ld
f**oo**t	

Exercise 2

Choose three words with /ʊ/ that you use frequently. Write typical sentences you might say with the words. Practice each sentence three times.

a. _____

b. _____

c. _____

Exercise 3

Repeat the word pairs in Listening Activity 3. Make a clear distinction between /ʊ/ and /uʷ/ and between /ʊ/ and /ʌ/.

Exercise 4

Practice the boldfaced, italicized words silently. Repeat the sentences. Look up from your book as you say each sentence.

a. I *couldn't* afford to buy the car.

b. We *should* apologize for the error.

c. *Would* you mind if I came late?

d. I *would* rather eat out than *cook*.

e. He *should* have been more careful.

f. I don't remember where I *put* my *books*.

g. The *football* stadium is *full*.

h. The candidate promised to *push* for tax reforms.

Exercise 5

Record yourself reading the paragraph titled "Eating Out" in Listening Activity 5 in the answer key. Monitor your pronunciation of underlined words with /ʊ/. Summarize the passage in your own words.

Communicative Practice

In groups of four to six, imagine that you are a member of a team of anthropologists. You have been asked to select seven items that represent popular culture today. These items will be placed in a time capsule to give people of the next century an idea of what life was like today.

Preview the phrases with /ʊ/ that are likely to occur during your discussion:

I think we *should* . . .

We *could* . . .

We need to include a *book* about . . .

We ought to *put* . . .

That *would*(n't) be a *good* choice . . .

Here are some suggestions to get you started:

Cell phone

Recycled paper product

Product label from a low-fat food item

Running shoes

Oprah Winfrey Book Club selection

5. Vowel 8: /ɑ/ as in *not* (vs. Vowel 11: /oʷ/ as in *no*)

Fact 1. The /ɑ/ is a pure vowel. The /oʷ/ glides upward toward a /w/ sound.

Fact 2. Students sometimes confuse /oʷ/ for /ɑ/ so that *rob* sounds like *robe* and *hope* sounds like *hop*.

Listening Activity 1

Listen to the /ɑ/ sound.

/ɑ/ ... /ɑ/ ... /ɑ/ ... /ɑ/ ... /ɑ/

Listen to /ɑ/ contrasted with /oʷ/.

/ɑ/ ... /oʷ/ ... /ɑ/ ... /oʷ/ ... /ɑ/ ... /oʷ/.

Listening Activity 2

Listen to the words with /ɑ/:

on, **o**ffer, j**o**b, n**o**t, sh**o**p, st**o**p, h**o**t, c**o**nduct (noun), s**o**lid, b**o**ttom, w**a**llet, f**a**ther

Listening Activity 3

Listen to the word pairs. Does the first or second word in each pair have the /ɑ/ sound? Close your book and write 1 or 2 on a separate piece of paper. Check the answer key.

a. not	note	**f.** odd	ode
b. cot	coat	**g.** soak	sock
c. stock	stoke	**h.** stoke	stock
d. cope	cop	**i.** con	cone
e. rob	robe	**j.** wrote	rot

Listening Activity 4

Listen to your teacher, the speaker on tape, or your partner say one of the prompts in each pair. Give the correct response. Check the answer key. As a pair practice, student 1 should cover responses, and student 2 should cover prompts.

PROMPTS (STUDENT 1)	RESPONSES (STUDENT 2)
a. He has a scar.	(From the accident.)
He has a score.	(From the game.)
b. Tell John it's snowing.	(He'll be excited.)
Tell Joan it's snowing.	(She'll be excited.)
c. Did you take care of the knots?	(Yes. I untied them.)
Did you take care of the notes?	(Yes. I mailed them.)

d. Did you get the cod?   (No. The market's out of fish.)

Did you get the code?   (No. The programmer's still
                                       working on it.)

Listening Activity 5

Listen to the paragraph. Fill in the blanks with words that have the /ɑ/ sound in stressed words and syllables. Check the answer key.

Jobs and Hormones

Testosterone, the hormone _____ for sex drive and aggression, may have

some influence on our choice of _____. According to a study by a Georgia

State University _____ professor, people with high levels of testosterone

_____ for professions in which they face severe competition to succeed.

Actors have the most testosterone of all; _____ and trial lawyers rank high too.

The lowest levels of testosterone are found among nurses and ministers, who devote

themselves to comforting, not competing with, others. Because women have lower

levels of testosterone than men in general, the researcher cautions that success is

_____ dependent on hormones. _____ is important, but it is not destiny.

Exercise 1

Repeat the words with /ɑ/.

on	c**o**st
odd	d**o**g
off	st**o**p
offer	sh**o**p
opposite	c**o**nfident
option	pr**o**bably
operate	f**o**llow
office	pr**o**duct

Exercise 2

Choose three words with /ɑ/ that you use frequently. Write typical sentences you might say with the words. Practice each sentence three times.

a. _____

b. _____

c. _____

Exercise 3

Repeat the word pairs in Listening Activity 3. Make a clear distinction between /ɑ/ and /oʷ/.

Exercise 4

Practice the boldfaced, italicized words silently. Repeat the sentences. Look up from your book as you say each sentence.

a. Which one *costs* the most?

b. *John* is doing his research in *robotics.*

c. The police *officer* caught the suspected *robber.*

d. There is a *lot* of *controversy* about *economic* recovery.

e. He *lost* a fortune in the *stock* market.

f. He's interested in *quality* control.

g. I'll *probably drop* it *off* on the way home.

h. The temperature should remain *constant.*

Exercise 5

Record yourself reading the paragraph titled "Jobs and Hormones" in Listening Activity 5 in the answer key. Monitor your pronunciation of the italicized words with /ɑ/. Summarize the mini-lecture in your own words.

Communicative Practice

What is important in a job? What motivates employees? Each student should rate the following criteria contributing to job satisfaction. Then select the three most important factors and the three least important factors.

In groups of three to five students, compare your answers. Did all agree on any of the criteria? What might account for differences of opinion? Did you rank the items from the perspective of an employee or a boss?

Preview words with /ɑ/ that are likely to occur during the discussion: *job, problems, opportunity, possibility, office, not, long, boss, cooperative.* Monitor /oʷ/ in these words: *most, promotion,* and *motivate.*

Factors Contributing to Job Satisfaction

How important are these factors?

	Very Important	Important	Slightly Important	Not at All Important
Good Salary				
Job Security				
Health Benefits				
Flexible Hours				
Opportunity for Leadership				
Participation in Decision-Making				
On-Site Day Care				
Being Your Own Boss				
Prestige				
Physical Activity				
Working with People				
Working with Your Mind				
Chance to Be Creative				
Length of Commute				

List the Three Most Important Factors

1. _____

2. _____

3. _____

List the Three Least Important Factors

1. _____

2. _____

3. _____

Answer Key for Appendix B

Voiced and Voiceless Consonants

Exercise 3		**Exercise 4**	
ri**p**	(ri**b**)	**v**iew	(**f**ew)
(we**d**)	we**t**	(**f**an)	**v**an
ri**ch**	(ri**dge**)	**b**ore	(**p**oor)
(ba**dge**)	ba**tch**	(a**pp**ear)	a **b**eer
fa**ce**	(pha**se**)	(**p**ack)	**b**ack
(le**d**)	le**t**	**g**lass	(**c**lass)
(plu**g**)	plu**ck**	(**c**ome)	**g**um
lea**f**	(lea**ve**)	**d**rip	(**t**rip)
hal**f**	(ha**ve**)	(**t**ime)	**d**ime
righ**t**	(ri**de**)	(**ch**eap)	**J**eep
(sa**ve**)	sa**fe**	(**ch**oke)	**j**oke
(play**s**)	pla**ce**		
sur**f**	(ser**ve**)		

Consonant 1: /θ/ as in *think*

Listening Activity 2

a. B	**d.** M	**g.** B	**j.** E
b. B	**e.** E	**h.** B	**k.** M
c. E	**f.** M	**i.** E	**l.** E

Listening Activity 3

a. 1	**d.** 1	**g.** 2	**i.** 2
b. 1	**e.** 2	**h.** 1	**j.** 1
c. 2	**f.** 1		

Listening Activity 4

a. It's not thick.

b. She wants to play baseball.

c. It's not a bush.

d. I'm almost certain she's two now.

e. He can't solve the problem alone.

Listening Activity 5

What Makes You Thin?

What makes you *thin?* Most people *think* that dieting is the answer, but researchers say that exercise is the best way to be *thin.* In one study, *thirty-two* men who were sedentary were put on an exercise program. They walked, jogged, and ran *throughout* the one-year program. The first *thing* the study showed was that the men who had exercised the most lost the most weight. The second *thing* the study revealed was that the men who lost the most weight ate more too. The researchers *theorize* that fat people don't really eat a lot. Their problem is that they are inactive.

Consonant 2: /f/ as in *fine*

Listening Activity 2

a. B	**d.** E	**g.** M	**j.** E
b. E	**e.** E	**h.** B	**k.** B
c. B	**f.** M	**i.** B	**l.** E

Listening Activity 3

a. 1	**d.** 2	**g.** 2	**j.** 2
b. 1	**e.** 2	**h.** 2	**k.** 1
c. 2	**f.** 1	**i.** 1	**l.** 1

Listening Activity 4

a. That's why the coffee tastes so good.

b. Do you have proof?

c. We never get raises.

d. Did you see her go by?

e. In the small appliances department.

Listening Activity 5

Videophones

In 1992, AT&T began **offering** customers a video**phone**, a **telephone** with a small color screen that allows callers to look at each other while they are talking. **If** callers **prefer** to be invisible, however, a special **feature** will close the lens of the camera. Now, in addition to the popular **phones** for your cars and video **telephone conferencing** systems that have become almost standard in the **offices** of big businesses, you can plug video**phones** into standard **telephone** outlets in your home.

Consonant 3: /ʃ/ as in *she*

Listening Activity 2

a. B	**d.** E	**g.** M	**i.** M
b. B	**e.** M	**h.** E	**j.** M
c. E	**f.** E		

Listening Activity 3

a. 1	**d.** 1	**g.** 1	**i.** 2
b. 1	**e.** 2	**h.** 2	**j.** 2
c. 2	**f.** 1		

Listening Activity 4

a. His sheets.

b. Should I put it in the refrigerator?

c. Sure. I used to play baseball.

d. She's in complete agreement.

Listening Activity 5

Shyness

About 92 million Americans are **shy**. Researchers are taking an interest in **shyness** and have reached different conclusions. According to one study, **social relations** these days are more complex, and **shyness** is becoming a **national** concern. Another study found that only about half of the **shy** people were tense or **anxious** in **social situations**, contrary to popular belief. And still another study found that **shy** people tend to be more stable in their **relationships**. Some psychologists think that **shyness** may be inherited, whereas others think that **shyness** is cultural.

Consonant 4: /r/ as in *right*

Listening Activity 2

a. B	**d.** E	**g.** M	**j.** M
b. B	**e.** M	**h.** M	**k.** M
c. E	**f.** B	**i.** E	**l.** B

Listening Activity 3

a. 1	**e.** 1	**i.** 2	**l.** 2
b. 1	**f.** 1	**j.** 2	**m.** 2
c. 2	**g.** 2	**k.** 1	**n.** 1
d. 1	**h.** 1		

Listening Activity 4

a. You need the short one.

b. At church.

c. In the sky.

d. He's holding a ball.

e. The leaves are killing the grass.

f. I like the Southwest.

Listening Activity 5

Butterflies in Your Stomach

If you've ever given a **report** in front of a class or a **group** of people, you know the feeling. Your heart **races,** your blood pressure **rises,** your hands start to shake, your throat gets **dry**, and you get **butter**flies in your stomach. What causes your body to **react** this way? When you're nervous or **frightened**, your glands **release** adrenaline into your bloodstream. The **adrenaline** causes your muscles to tense up. It also causes **increased** motion in your stomach muscles. As a **result**, your stomach **produces** more acid than it needs for digestion. The acid feels like **butter**flies in your stomach.

Consonant 5: /v/ as in *vote*

Listening Activity 2

a. B		**d.** E		**g.** M		**i.** E	
b. B		**e.** B		**h.** B		**j.** M	
c. M		**f.** M					

Listening Activity 3

a. 1		**e.** 2		**i.** 1		**l.** 2	
b. 1		**f.** 1		**j.** 2		**m.** 1	
c. 2		**g.** 1		**k.** 2		**n.** 1	
d. 1		**h.** 1					

Listening Activity 4

a. On the bike.

b. A dry red wine.

c. They remind me of her.

d. The engine died.

e. He loves to ride waves.

Listening Activity 5

Valentine's Day

For *over* 100 years, it has been popular to *give* cards, flowers, gifts, and other tokens of *love* on February 14, St. Valentine's Day in the United States. There are *several* explanations for the origin of this holiday; *however*, the most believable is that St. *Valentine's* Day is a *survival* of a February 15th Roman festival. During this *festival*, bachelors picked names of women to *discover* who their *"valentines"* or *lovers* would be for the coming year. The couples then exchanged gifts and sometimes *even* became engaged.

Answer Key for Appendix C

1. Vowel 2: /ɪ/ as in *hit*

Listening Activity 3

a. 1	**d.** 2	**g.** 2	**i.** 1
b. 1	**e.** 2	**h.** 1	**j.** 2
c. 2	**f.** 1		

Listening Activity 4

a. Yes, on the ice.

b. It was a good crop.

c. Yes. She's packing her bags now.

d. Yes, with the hammer.

e. In the medicine chest.

Listening Activity 5

Drinking and Health Risks

People often *lift* a glass to toast good health. *Drinking* may indeed lower the *risk* of several diseases, according to some interesting *statistics* released by the Harvard School of Public Health. Researchers found that up to one to two *drinks* each day diminished the *risk* of heart attack, stroke, and fatal heart disease by about twenty-*six* percent in men and up to *fifty* percent in *women.* One researcher warned, however, that women with a family *history* of breast cancer should *limit* drinking because alcohol is *linked* to a higher risk of breast cancer.

2. Vowel 4: /ɛ/ as in *met*

Listening Activity 3

a. 2	**d.** 1	**g.** 1	**j.** 1
b. 2	**e.** 2	**h.** 2	**k.** 2
c. 1	**f.** 1	**i.** 1	**l.** 2

Listening Activity 4

a. For dinner tonight.

b. I'm sorry you missed him.

c. It was too spicy.

d. Did you like him?

e. Nice and sharp.

Listening Activity 5

Airbags

The airbag has become standard equipment in every new car. It is stored in the *center* of the steering wheel and, in an accident, quickly inflates to *help* save a driver's life. But how does it work? The airbag has electronic *sensors* that can feel a crash as it begins to happen. The sensors *set* off a small can of nitrogen gas, which rushes into the bag. The soft bag *protects* the driver and *then* it deflates. Airbags are only useful in *head*-on or rear-*end* accidents. During a side collision, a driver needs a seat *belt* for protection.

3. Vowel 7: /ʌ/ as in *nut*

Listening Activity 3

a. 2   **d.** 1   **g.** 1   **i.** 2

b. 2   **e.** 1   **h.** 1   **j.** 1

c. 1   **f.** 2

Listening Activity 4

a. Yes. It has fur.

b. For coffee.

c. I hate that shade of green.

d. I can't untie it.

e. No. I lost.

Listening Activity 5

Foreign-Born Numbers Are Up

In a 1997 **study**, the Census Bureau reports that nearly **one** in 10 residents of the United States was foreign born. The number is nearly **double** the percentage of foreign born in 1970 (4.8%). **Much** of the foreign-born population—one third of all immigrants—resides in California. New York ranks second and Florida third. The **government** study also includes where immigrants are **from.** One of every two foreign–born residents **comes** from Central and South America and the Caribbean.

Communicative Practice

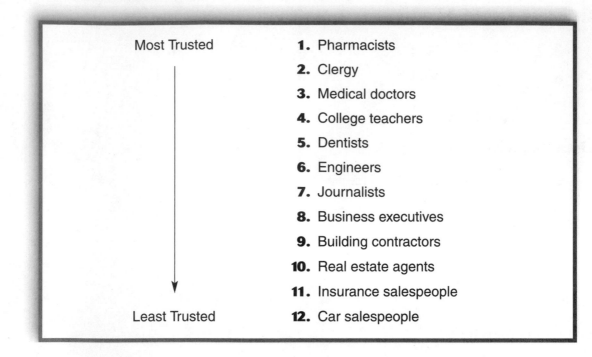

Most Trusted

1. Pharmacists
2. Clergy
3. Medical doctors
4. College teachers
5. Dentists
6. Engineers
7. Journalists
8. Business executives
9. Building contractors
10. Real estate agents
11. Insurance salespeople

Least Trusted   12. Car salespeople

4. Vowel 10: /ʊ/ as in *took*

Listening Activity 3

a. 1   **c.** 2   **e.** 2   **g.** 1

b. 2   **d.** 1   **f.** 1   **h.** 2

Listening Activity 4

a. It's all over the fireplace.

b. He'll have to swim someplace else.

c. It needs to cool.

d. To the cleaners.

Listening Activity 5

Eating Out

People in the United States are spending less time **cooking** and more time eating out in restaurants. In fact, many people in the United States eat out on the average of four times a week. If you invite someone to join you for dinner in a restaurant, here are some general guidelines. You **should** phone first to find out whether you need a reservation. When you invite someone out to dinner, you **should** be prepared to pay the bill. However, sometimes the guests **would** rather pay so that they won't feel indebted to you. When the bill arrives, **look** to see whether the tip has been added to the cost of the food. Most restaurants do not add the tip to the bill. You **should** leave a tip equal to 15 percent of the bill if the service was adequate. If the restaurant is expensive or if the service was especially **good**, you **could** leave up to 20 percent of the bill.

5. Vowel 8: /ɑ/ as in *not*

Listening Activity 3

a. 1	**d.** 2	**g.** 2	**i.** 1
b. 1	**e.** 1	**h.** 2	**j.** 2
c. 1	**f.** 1		

Listening Activity 4

a. From the accident.

b. He'll be excited.

c. Yes. I mailed them.

d. No. The market's out of fish.

Listening Activity 5

Jobs and Hormones

Testosterone, the hormone **responsible** for sex drive and aggression, may have some influence on our choice of **jobs.** According to a study by a Georgia State University **psychology** professor, people with high levels of testosterone **opt** for professions in which they face severe competition to succeed. Actors have the most testosterone of all; **doctors** and trial lawyers rank high too. The lowest levels of testosterone are found among nurses and ministers, who devote themselves to comforting, not competing with, others. Because women have lower levels of testosterone than men in general, the researcher cautions that success is **not** dependent on hormones. **Biology** is important, but it is not destiny.

Index